speaker at 2018 all church camp at Ghost Ranch

PREACHING CREATION

PREACHING CREATION

The Environment and the Pulpit

John C. Holbert

CASCADE *Books* · Eugene, Oregon

PREACHING CREATION
The Environment and the Pulpit

Cascade Books
A Division of Wipf and Stock Publishers
199 W. 8th Ave., Suite 3
Eugene, OR 97401

www.wipfandstock.com

Some scripture quotations are from the *King James Version* of the Bible, first published in 1611.

Some scripture quotations are from *The Revised Standard Version* of the Bible, copyright 1946, 1952, and 1971 by the Division of Christian Education of the National Council of Churches.

Some scripture quotations are from *The Jerusalem Bible*, copyright © 1966, 1967, and 1968 by Darton, Longman & Todd Ltd and Doubleday and Company, Inc.

Scripture quotations from the *New Revised Standard Version* of the Bible and copyright © 1989 by the Division of Christian Education of the National Council of the Churches of Christ in the U.S.A. and are used by permission.

Cataloging-in-Publication data:

Holbert, John C.

    Preaching creation : the environment and the pulpit / John C. Holbert.

    vi + 114 p. ; 23 cm. Includes bibliographical references.

    ISBN 13: 978-1-61097-379-3

    1. Ecology—Christianity. 2. Bible. O.T.—Criticism, interpretation, etc. 3. Bible. N.T.—Criticism, interpretation, etc. 4. Homiletics. 5. Sermons—American. I. Title.

BT695.5 H665 2011

Manufactured in the U.S.A.

Contents

Introduction

A March morning is only as drab as he who walks in it without a glance
skyward, ear cocked for geese. I once knew an educated lady, banded by Phi
Beta Kappa, who told me that she had never heard or seen the geese that twice
a year proclaim the revolving seasons to her well-insulated roof. Is education
possibly a process for trading awareness for things of lesser worth? The goose
who trades his is soon a pile of feathers.

—ALDO LEOPOLD

WE ARE LIVING IN a modern world faced with ecological degradation—
deforestation, rapid species extinction, ozone depletion, greenhouse
warming, to name but a few of the monsters that stalk our twenty-first-
century landscapes. In Leopold's grim metaphor, we appear to be trading
awareness of these imminent dangers for things of lesser worth. Like his
unaware goose, we might quickly become only a pile of feathers. But we
Christians are by nature a people of hope. Indeed it could be said that we
are by definition hopeful people; a Christian pessimist is nothing else than
an oxymoron.

Still, it would be very easy to become a pessimist in the face of the
monumental challenges we face. Air, soil, forests, oceans, drinking water:
resource depletion on every side. The wrong things are rising: temperatures, oceans, carbon content in the air; and the wrong things are falling:
rain forests, water tables, oil and natural gas reserves. We are clearly on a
head-on collision course between our desires and our resources to fulfill
them. The example of global warming will make the point.

Though there remain a few straggling politicians and a few scientists who are not convinced of the human impact on the rising temperatures of the earth, their numbers are fast decreasing. A 2002 Republican strategy memo from Frank Luntz is becoming an anomaly. "Voters believe there is no consensus about global warming in the scientific community. Should the public come to believe that the scientific issues are settled, their views about global warming will change accordingly . . . The scientific debate is closing (against us) but not yet closed. There is still a window of opportunity to challenge the science."[1] In the eight years since Mr. Luntz gave this advice to the Republican administration for which he worked, I would suggest that the scientific debate window has closed almost completely. Even the president at that time, George W. Bush, who early in his first term publicly doubted the proof of global warming, was quoted at the G-8 summit in Gleneagles, Scotland, July 2005, as saying that he now believed that human industrial activity over the past two hundred years had indeed contributed to the worldwide rise in temperatures. Unfortunately, he still refused to affix his signature to the Kyoto treaty on global warming, the only comprehensive treaty on the problem. The treaty took effect on Feb 16, 2005, having been signed by more than 130 of the world's countries.

Earlier in 2005, a remarkable study appeared. The study was done in an attempt to demonstrate the existence of global warming as a result of human industrial activity. A British researcher, David Stainforth, asked 95,000 volunteers from 150 countries to run over 60,000 simulations on climate change on their personal computers.[2] A lengthy list of variables, both atmospheric and oceanic, was used in the simulations, and the initial report was based on analysis of about 2,000 of those simulations. The results were sobering. The average of the simulations predicted a temperature rise of six degrees Fahrenheit over the next one hundred years, though some suggested as high as twenty degrees. Even if the rise is only 3.6 degrees above the average temperature of 1750, the beginning of the Industrial Revolution, the impact on the world would be appalling. The report says, "[Such a rise] and the risks to human societies and ecosystems grow significantly," leading to the danger of "abrupt, accelerated, or runaway climate change."[3] Results of such changes would be the melting

1. Talking Points, *The Dallas Morning News*, May 15, 2005.
2. Full details of this study are available at *climateprediction.net*.
3. Associated Press, "Study rethinks risk of greenhouse gases," *The Dallas Morning*

of the West Antarctic and Greenland ice sheets; the shutting down of the Gulf Stream; the enormous rise in ocean heights with resulting flooding, loss of human, animal, and plant life; and on and on.

The report goes on to say that such a temperature rise can be avoided by keeping the concentration of carbon dioxide in the atmosphere below 400 parts per million. Current concentrations are on average 379 parts per million though most recent measurements put the figure at 390.[4] "Business as usual," if no changes are made in human habits—carbon-based fuel consumption as the chief culprit—will result in a future of dystopian horror. This problem of global warming is merely one among many environmental tipping points that we face as a world. With problems of such magnitude, the church's voice must be heard. And when the church speaks, its voice is empowered by the texts of the Bible.

Unfortunately, the history of the Bible's use as a text for a more hopeful ecology is checkered at best. It cannot be denied that Genesis' claim that God gave humanity "dominion" over fish, bird, and every sort of land creature, and further commanded that they "subdue" the earth that God had given them (Gen 1:26, 28), has led believers to the most appalling sorts of ecological assault. Religious and philosophical discussion in England during the rise of the industrial revolution in the eighteenth century pointed all too often to texts from the Bible as warrants for unfettered economic exploitation of the earth.[5] Similarly in the United States preachers and theologians either silently acquiesced to environmental abuse as the nation's economic engines began to roar, or, worse, they egged those engines on with biblical exhortations to "tame the frontier" for human settlement and ever-increasing comforts.[6]

Then in the middle of the nineteenth century there arose the significant movement known as modern millenarianism. Based on a particular

---

News, January 30, 2005. See now the more extensive treatment of the imminent dangers of rising temperatures in Hertsgaard, *Hot: Living Through the Next Fifty Years on Earth*.

4. Associated Press, "Study rethinks risks of greenhouse gases," *The Dallas Morning News*, Jan 30, 2005.

5. See Santmire, *The Travail of Nature*, 133–43, for a brief overview of the writing that addresses science and the environment from the seventeenth to the nineteenth centuries in England.

6. See Wirzba, *The Paradise of God*, for a lyrical and subtle recounting of the rise of technology in the West and the denial of creation that resulted, especially his chapter 2, "Culture as the Denial of Creation," 61–92.

reading of the Bible, pioneered by the Englishman John Nelson Darby, called dispensationalism, the Bible was seen as a book of prediction, wherein one could read the course of the world's future. This belief and its implications have survived until today as premillenialism.[7] In such a reading, at the end of the sixth dispensation (the time in which we are supposedly now living) there will occur the "rapture of the church"—that is, all true believers will be rescued from an increasingly evil earth. After this rapture there will arise the great tribulation where the Antichrist will reign and millions will die under his terror. Then just before the final battle of Armageddon in Israel, Jesus will return with his raptured church and will defeat the forces of the Antichrist. Those who convert to belief in him will be saved from death, but all those who do not will be killed and sent to hell.

What all this speculative drama has to do with our subject of the environment can be summarized by a quotation from D.L. Moody, one of the leading premillenialists of the late nineteenth century, and founder of the Moody Bible Institute, which still exists in Chicago.

> I look on this world as a wrecked vessel. God has given me a life-boat, and said to me, "Moody, save all you can." God will come in judgment and burn up this world, but the children of God don't belong to this world; they are in it, but not of it, like a ship in the water. The world is getting darker and darker; its ruin is coming nearer and nearer. If you have any friends on this wreck unsaved, you had better lose no time in getting them off.[8]

The earth on which we live is unalterably evil, and God has it in mind to destroy it and take those who love God to a better place in heaven. This idea of an evil earth, a place of darkness, chaos, and sin, is central to these end-time scenarios. And these biblical views are shared by millions of Americans in the twenty-first century, as every poll suggests. Thus, our earth is not to be loved, since it inevitably will be destroyed by God, and all who truly love God will be transported to a better place. The implication for those who would love the earth, and would work for its betterment, is

---

7. Excellent histories of this important movement in nineteenth- and twentieth-century America may be found in Weber, *Living in the Shadow of the Second Coming;* Boyer, *When Time Shall Be No More*; and Weber, *On the Road to Armageddon.*

8. Quoted in Weber, *Living in the Shadow,* 53.

obvious: why waste your time? It will all be gone someday anyway, since that is the biblical will of God.

Thus, both an earth-hating millenarianism, and an overtly cozy relationship between public Christianity and unchecked economic growth, accompanied by an increasingly unhealthy environment, ultimately caused Lynn White, Jr. to write a much-quoted article, "The Historical Roots of Our Ecological Crisis," in 1967.[9] In that article, White said that Genesis 1:28's claim that God had commanded humanity to "subdue" the earth, coupled with the idea that Christianity had destroyed the notion that there was a sacred presence within nature, made possible the scientific and technological attack, along with the millenarian theological attack, on the natural environment.

> In antiquity, every tree, every spring, every stream, every hill had its own *genius loci*, its guardian spirit. . . . Before one cut a tree, mined a mountain, or dammed a brook, it was important to placate the spirit in charge of that particular institution, and to keep it placated. By destroying pagan animism, Christianity made it possible to exploit nature in a mood of indifference to the feelings of natural objects.[10]

Despite the import of this quotation, White was not suggesting that we modern Christians return to some sort of animism. On the contrary, he argued that the seeds of a healthy ecological theology lay in the history of Christianity itself. He urged another look at St. Francis of Assisi, called by White "the greatest spiritual revolutionary in western history."[11] What Christians need, concluded White, is the "substitution of the idea of the equality of all creatures, including man, for the idea of man's limitless rule of creation."[12] Francis attempted this substitution, but his radical idea failed to gain significant support in the church.

White's article has undergone forty years of probing critique. Questions have been raised concerning his selective and limited understanding of the Bible's rich discussions of creation theology, his claim that Christianity especially made scientific and technological revolu-

9. Reprinted many times, but first published in *Science*.

10. White, 132, as found in Granberg-Michaelson, *Ecology and Life*.

11. White, 137. For similar sentiments about Francis and the church's missed opportunity, see Santmire, *The Travail*, 106–19.

12. Ibid.

tions possible, and that it was uniquely western culture that spawned environmental destruction. It is hardly surprising that one short article, purposely polemic in tone, would prick numerous critics from the various fields of study addressed. Nevertheless, the fact that the article is still read, discussed, and quoted suggests that White struck a nerve. Is his claim accurate that Christianity, and the Judaism that preceded it, are anti-environmental? If so, would we be better off with some other construal of reality than the Christian one? In a word, I think the answer is No. But we do need, I also think, another way to construe Christianity and its relationship to the creation of God.

The purpose of this book is not specifically to critique Lynn White's understanding of Christianity's rendering of creation. However, it will become clear enough that I think White's construal of biblical ideas of creation is in the main quite wrong. Still, it is important to know that this book's purpose is more than contrarian. The goal, rather, is to examine selected portions of the Hebrew Bible and the New Testament, in order to enumerate, at least in outline, just what this ancient literature has to say about this crucial subject.

But I have more in mind than that. The great majority of the book's readers will be preachers, those who attempt week by week to illuminate the ancient texts so as to shine a probing light on modern hearers. Thus, my reflections on the Bible's ideas of creation will be accompanied by suggestions for preaching those ideas. After all, ideas are only abstract constructs until they are released into the ears of those who would, or need, to hear.

I have chosen eight portions of tradition for more detailed analysis, five from the Hebrew Bible and three from the New Testament. My choices are to a certain extent arbitrary; there are many other texts that cry out for explication. Still, I believe the chosen texts are important ones for the subject, and that a careful, though necessarily too brief, exegesis of them will generate significant insights for those of us who want to grasp more fully what the written Word of God has to say in this matter of the creation. Each chapter will be accompanied by a sermon on the text under examination. The sermons are designed to offer diverse ways that a preacher might approach this particular subject in a sermon; they are hardly normative, but merely suggestive for your own preaching.

Books are born in many ways. This one was my own idea, and another press agreed to have me write it. But due to other commitments, and quite frankly a cooling of my own interest in the project, I voided the initial contract and put the work aside. But further reading, reflection, and an increasing awareness that this subject was a crucial one for the church, rekindled my interest, and the book you hold is the fruit of that renewed enthusiasm.

Now let me add what may seem an odd dedication. I write this for our own spaceship earth, that wondrous craft that carries us in our cycles around the tiny star fueling our miniscule part of God's universe. Some believe that earth to be a living organism, ever-breathing, ever-changing under and around us. Whether or not it actually is alive in that way, it makes it possible for us to live. Yet, we can "kill" it, too, and thus ourselves, unless we take more seriously what the ancient, pre-scientific texts tried to say about our relationship to it. The time to act is now, for we face vast problems that cannot wait. We preachers must play our role. We must preach about the love of God's creation, both in order to honor God but also to help preserve the magnificent gift that God has given.

I am asking for nothing less than a conversion in our thinking about the Bible and its commitments to earth. My own thinking has been transformed by my work on this topic with the help of many capable thinkers from the biblical, theological, and scientific fields. It is crucial that we preachers get this subject right, because issues of ecology, resource use, climate change, and a host of other related topics will soon become, if they already are not now, the most important cluster of concerns that we humans are facing. It will not merely be helpful if you wrestle with these ideas in your preaching; it will be vital for the future of the cosmos. I want to call us to change, that is all of us who preach and all of us who hear. We must preach and hear as if our lives depended on it, because in the case of our relationship to the creation, they do.

1

"In the Beginning"

Genesis and Creation

The point of the dragonfly's terrible lip, the giant water bug, birdsong, or the beautiful dazzle and flash of sun-lighted minnows, is not that it all fits together like clockwork—for it doesn't, particularly, not even inside the goldfish bowl—but that it all flows so freely wild, like the creek, that it all surges in such a free, fringed tangle. Freedom is the world's water and weather, the world's nourishment freely given, its soil and sap: and the creator loves pizzazz.

—ANNIE DILLARD

FEW PORTIONS OF THE biblical record have generated more comment than the poetry that comprises the opening chapter of Genesis. Theologians, scientists (and pseudo-scientists), sociologists, anthropologists, mythologists all have turned their steady gaze at these ancient words. Amazingly, even in our twenty-first century more than a few judges and lawyers are confronted again and again with plaintiffs who are insistent that Genesis 1 is science, pure and simple, and ought to be so taught. Yet, others say just as passionately that Genesis 1 is not science at all, but is rather theology dressed in poetry.[1] To be clear from the outset, I hold with the latter thinkers. Genesis 1 is poetic theology. It is not science in any modern sense. More precisely it is essentially one thing: it is doxology, announcing and celebrating the truth that God creates and is creating.

Doxology

For those of us who read the Bible as the ancient and inspired reflections of persons asking the most basic questions of human and divine life, the words of Genesis 1 do not attempt to prove anything. The author holds no theory subject to some supposed canon of science. I am not challenged by the chapter's words to perform experiments in order to prove the findings of the chapter. When I finish reading or hearing the chapter, I am asked to accept its claims as the basis on which I should live my life. In short, Genesis 1 is doxology, literally the "study of glory."

The best analogy is found in that doxological act that many worshippers perform in services of worship, usually after the acceptance of the monetary offering. All who are able stand and sing some form of "Praise God from Whom All Blessings Flow." We do this to remind ourselves that the money we have just given for the work of the church, for the work of God that we pray that the church performs, is not our money at all, at least not in any ultimate sense. Since all blessings flow from God, we sing, then we should live our lives according to that truth. In the same way in Genesis 1, by saying "In beginning God created sky and earth," we affirm that God is creator, the founding entity of our universe. I am not creator; at most I can only be co-creator. However one understands that relationship, the world belongs to God, as Psalm 24 so memorably hymns. The Genesis chapter merely "states" the truth, and does not attempt to prove it.

---

1. The twentieth century German theologian, Karl Barth, made this point in an especially delightful way. In a letter to his grandniece, Christine Barth, on February 18, 1965, responding to a question she had asked, he spoke about the supposed relationships between Genesis and evolution:

> Has no one explained to you in your seminar that one can as little compare the biblical creation story and a scientific theory like that of evolution as one can compare, shall we say, an organ and a vacuum cleaner—that there is as little question as harmony between them as of contradiction. *Karl Barth Letters* 1961–1968, 184.

If I may add a bit to the great theologian's whimsical analogy, I would say that both organ and vacuum cleaner use wind, but for very different and very incompatible purposes.

That is essentially why Genesis 1 is Genesis 1. The Bible begins with a forceful announcement of the nature and purpose of the God who will be the chief actor and director of the drama about to unfold. Above all, says Gen 1, this God is creator, the fashioner of all that is. From sky to earth, from water to land, from sun to moon to stars, from plants with visible seeds to plants with hidden seeds, from wild creatures (lions, tigers, and bears, oh my!), to domesticated creatures (dogs, cats, and horses), to male and female human beings, the Lord God made them all. And all from the hand of that God is good. The chapter celebrates, in the probable form of a liturgical responsive reading, the creative energies of God. As God is encountered in the rest of the biblical story, the fact of God's initial exuberant creation can never be forgotten. Hence the hallmark of the first chapter of Genesis is doxology.

And the more specific concern of God's creation, what has often been called the apogee of God's creative arc, is found in the human creation of verses 26–28. (Unless otherwise stated, the translations of the Bible are my own.)

> (26) God said, "Let us make a human being in our image,
> just like our likeness, and let them rule over the fish in
> the sea and the birds of the skies, as well as the domesticated
> and wild creatures that move across the land." (27) So God created
> the human being in God's image; in the image of God God
> created it; male and female God created them. (28) Then God
> blessed them and said to them, "Be fruitful! Increase! Fill the
> land and subdue it. Rule over the fish in the sea, the birds of the
> skies, as well as the living things that move across the land."

These three short verses are crammed with wonder and packed with potential problems of understanding.[2] For our present purposes, four issues will be addressed.

2. Standard commentaries include: Von Rad, *Genesis*, 57–61; Westermann, *Genesis 1–11*, 142–61; Brueggemann, *Genesis*, 31–35; Vawter, *On Genesis*, 50–60; and *Ancient Christian Commentary on Scripture, Old Testament*, Genesis 1–11, 27–41.

The image and likeness of God

Gallons of ink (and now millions of bytes) have been used to explicate what these metaphors may suggest. The Hebrew for "image" is *tselem*. It is a relatively rare word in the Bible (fifteen uses), but its common thread is that it always means a physical representation of something (e.g., in 1 Samuel 6:5 and 2 Kings 11:18). The word "likeness" is *demuth*. This word has as its primary meaning a quality or condition. Even in the light of this evidence, many commentators have quickly announced that the verse surely does not imply that human creation is to be seen as physically resembling God. Yet, the loss of that element of the metaphor is dangerous. If I can actually imagine that each human being I see is in some remarkable sense the spitting image of God, would I not treat that person as more valuable, literally more God-like, than I might if I think of them as only somehow spiritually in God's image?

Thus, the man on the park bench downtown, wearing ragged clothes, smelling of the streets, drinking from a bottle hidden in a brown paper bag, is made directly in God's image as I am. The first lesson of God's human creation is then one of equality in God; all are made in the image of God.

The "plurality" of God's creation

It has long been a conundrum for readers of Gen 1 to see the three plural references in the person of God in verse 26. Various answers have been given.

A. The reference is mythological. All cultures surrounding Israel had multiple gods in their representations of divine reality. Here is an older reference to such a view not fully expunged from the written tradition. Fretheim speaks of an "inner-divine consultation"[3] By this he appears to mean that YHWH[4] is consulting with a divine court of beings, here un-

---

3. Fretheim, *God and World*, 42.

4. I will transcribe the "divine tetragrammaton," the four consonants of the ancient Israelite name for God, as YHWH. The New Revised Standard Version (NRSV) of the Bible reads the name as LORD, based an an older Jewish practice of reading YHWH as *'adonai*, Hebrew for "lord." Because the Hebrews grew reluctant to say the name of their God aloud, using that euphemism "lord," I suggest that YHWH preserves the unpro-

named, as is described in Job 1-2; 1 Kings 22:19; and Isaiah 6:1-8. Because this consultative role is used only in the human creation, and not for other objects of the creation, Fretheim concludes "we are led to expect that God will involve human beings in the creative process in some way"[5]

B. The reference is to a "royal we." As royalty in later times, or as the pope in Rome still does, persons of special power refer to themselves as "we," indicating that they are more than a single individual, but speak for many in their individual address.

C. Early Christian commentators saw here a very early reference to the Holy Trinity. God in creation was speaking in the Trinity of the Godhead. After all, it was reasoned, in the Gospel of John, and the epistles of Colossians and Hebrews, the preexistent nature of Christ was explicitly affirmed.

D. Some Jewish commentators suggested that God was speaking to the angels (Genesis Rabbah 8.5). While the angels argued for and against the human creation, God went ahead and did it anyway, and told the angels to be quiet![6]

E. Is it possible that God was speaking to the just-created animals when the decision to create humans was made? Hence, the humans were from the very beginning made a little like God and a little like beasts. This charming and suggestive idea raises interesting notions about the nature of humanity: we are as much God as we are beast. And it could be said that the latter part of our nature too often gets the upper hand.

It should be noted that the only one of these answers to the question of the plural references to take account of the text as we have it is the last one. The first four all import into their answers ideologies from outside the text itself. Answer E alone tries to take seriously the text we have. In that light, this delightful possibility needs to be taken with seriousness. In a discussion of God's human creation, the idea that humans are both God and beast could lead to fruitful reflection on our creation and its

nounceble mystery of the name.

5. Fretheim, *God and World*, 43.

6. Noted in the *Jewish Study Bible*, Michael Fishbane, 14.

nature and purpose. And the dual image of humanity could serve to bind us closer to the animals that share our planet with us.

What does it mean to "rule over"?

This powerful verb has been one of the sticking points in the attempt to understand what Gen 1 has to say about the function of human creation. There can be little question that this verb regularly means "to dominate," often harshly. In Leviticus 25:43, 46, and 53, in the great chapter describing the jubilee of land and freedom, Israel is warned "not to rule harshly" over fellow Israelites who have fallen into poverty and debt-slavery. In the next chapter, at Leviticus 26:17, that same Israel is warned that disobedience of God's commands will result in other nation's harsh rule over them! Likewise in Ezekiel's excoriation of Israel's false leaders (bad shepherds, he calls them), one of the charges against them is "harsh ruling," rather than healing the sick, binding up the wounded, and seeking the lost (Ezek 34:4). Indeed, these so-called leaders have failed to do what the two coronation Psalms 72:8 and 110:2 say rulers of Israel must do: they must "rule" but with "justice" and "righteousness" (also Ps 78:1).

So, the evidence of the use of the verb implies that harshness and domination are not finally inevitable consequences of the verb's meaning. Just as the king in the Psalms is commanded, so are the human beings in Genesis commanded to rule over God's creation. And the element of justice and righteousness enters into Genesis with the claim that humanity is made in the image of God.

The God who tames the mighty waters of chaos in order that the dry land appear, who shapes sun, moon, and stars, who forms plants of wondrous kinds and creatures of every variety, is a God of ordering, structuring, and designing. It is that God in whose image we all are made. In the last analysis, the *imago dei*, the image of the God of order, is what calls Lynn White's polemic against the Genesis worldview into the most serious question.[7]

When God commands human beings to rule over the created world, that command is regulated by the earlier announcement that we act as humans made directly in God's image. We are God's agents and are commanded to act in ways we discern that God acts. The best word perhaps

7. See the comments in the Introduction concerning the White article.

we can use to describe this divine action is the Hebrew *shalom*. Though it is often thought that the word means "peace," in reality its basic meaning is "wholeness/unity." A movement toward shalom is a movement away from fragmentation and disharmony. To claim that the Hebrew world-view necessarily fragments human beings from the created order is to misunderstand what God's action in creation was and is. God orders and so we order; God shapes for good and so we shape for good. Our assault against our environment is a direct assault against the good order of God and a direct denial of our creation as God's human image. We rule over God's creation only insofar as we remember that we are God's human images. When we forget that, we are rogue beasts, allowing that part of our created nature to mask the divine part, that part that commands us to live in harmony and oneness with each other and with the rest of creation. However much we have distorted the rich understanding of "dominion in God's image," this appears to be what the authors of Gen 1 affirmed.

Mark Brett adds some helpful reflections to the verses, claiming that the text itself is fully aware that human rule is very easily and regularly distorted by the more bestial side of our natures.[8] When God commands humans to "rule over," the language of kingship is introduced. However mixed the portraits of the rule of kings in the Bible, many of the pictures being very negative, primarily kings are to rule "in justice and righteousness," giving special attention to the poor and oppressed (see especially Ps 72:2, 4, 12–14). However, the subsequent command to "subdue" adds a contrastive understanding of human rule. Brett suggests that the possibly "utopian" notion of a humanity completely committed to care for the weak, is now "marked by a significant tension, which probably betrays the realities of daily experience in the ancient world."[9] Ideally we are to rule in the image of God; in reality we too often subdue for our own less-than-divine purposes. A closer look at the language of "subduing" will be instructive.

What does it mean to "dominate/subdue?"

The verb is most commonly used when the enemies of Israel, who lived in the land of promise, have been "subdued" by God (see Num 32:22, 29;

8. Mark G. Brett, "Earthing the Human in Genesis 1–3," 73–79.

9 Ibid., 78.

Josh 18:1; 2 Sam 8:11). Jeremiah 34:11, 16 admonishes those Israelites who reject the command of their king to free their Israelite slaves by forcing ("subduing") them back into slavery. Also, King Ahasuerus is horrified when he thinks he sees Haman "subduing" (forcing?) his queen, Esther, on his own couch after a meal attended by all three (Esth 7:8).

It appears that the human beings are commanded to "dominate/subdue" the rest of creation in the same manner that God prepared the Promised Land by subduing the enemies of Israel. There is no question that this image is a troublesome one. God's treatment of Israel's enemies has often been judged harsh and appalling; are we now commanded to act as God has acted?

Again, the command must be seen in the bright light of the image of the God of creation, the God of *shalom*. If we are to act as agents in God's world, we can do so only if we understand how God has acted in the creation of that world. In this first chapter of Genesis, it is completely inappropriate to view God's created order as the enemy of humanity. Still, some of that order is dangerous to humanity. It was in the ancient world always a tightrope act to live in God's good world with creatures that would kill and destroy if they were not "subdued." The question will always arise: who has a right to determine which creatures have priority in God's world? Is it the case that because I have the most developed brain, and have the power of reasoned speech, that I am the most important creature in the world of God? The very structure of Genesis 1, with the human creation placed at the end of the acts of God, suggests that that is exactly what the writers thought.

But the dangers for us and for nature in such a reading are obvious. If I take those verbs quite literally, and quite apart from my creation in God's image, then I might well "rule" and "subdue" for selfish and monstrously destructive ends. The human relationship to the created order has too often been characterized by just such a dangerous reading. In that respect Lynn White is not wrong: the havoc he has witnessed with respect to the creation is in part precisely the result of terribly perverse readings of the texts of Genesis 1. Still, these words are a significant part of the first chapter of Genesis, in some ways the crowning activity of God's good creation. What are those of us who love and preach the Bible to do?

One important way to deal with the problematically harsh language of Genesis 1:26–28 is to add to the portrait of human creation the words of Genesis 2:15. It is quite clear that the material of Genesis 2 arises from different sources than that of Genesis 1, a fact long affirmed in the study of the Hebrew Bible. However, the fact that both accounts were kept alive in the tradition, both being preserved in the canonical text, suggests that both can play a significant role in any formulation of a fuller exegetical understanding. Genesis 2:15 provides an important counter-weight to the picture of Genesis 1:26–28.

Unfortunately, the traditional translation of the verse is problematic and finally misleading. The King James Version (KJV) of 1611 reads: "And the LORD God took the man, and put him into the Garden of Eden to *dress* it and to keep it." The 1951 Revised Standard Version (RSV) has: "The LORD God took the man and put him in the Garden of Eden to *till* it and to keep it."(The 1989 NRSV reads the same.) The 1966 Jerusalem Bible (JB) reads: "Yahweh God took the man and settled him in the garden of Eden to *cultivate* and take care of it." These three translations are representative of the common ways that the Hebrew verb *'abad* has been rendered. The basic meaning of the word is "to serve," and from the verb arises the common noun "slave" or "servant." It is no accident that translators for four hundred years have used words that reflect human action *on* the garden, since under the influence of Genesis 1:26–28 we humans are given dominion; we are the actors on the creation. Hence, we "dress" or "till" or "cultivate" the garden of God. We are God's stewards, God's gardeners, dressers, tillers.

Frankly, this long-held metaphor has failed. Our relationship to God's earth, God's garden, has not been one of stewardship but one of assault and attack. The harshness of the verbs of Genesis 1:26–28 has been played out in our abuse of creation. It is past time to retire the metaphors of dominion and its partner, stewardship, and replace it with a more natural translation of Genesis 2:15. We now need to read: "The LORD God took the *'adam* and placed it[10] in the garden of Eden to serve it and to protect it."[11] Such a change has crucial implications for the human relationship to creation.

---

10. I translate the pronoun "it," referring to the *'adam*, rather than "him" because sexual differentiation in the story does not occur until the creation of the woman at 2:22. Thus the *'adam* becomes man and woman, but initially has no sexuality. See Phyllis Trible, *God and the Rhetoric of Sexuality*, 78–80.

11. Santmire, *Nature Reborn*, 122.

When we translate the verb "till" or "cultivate," we imply directly that nature always serves us; it has no intrinsic value. We are always the actors on creation, since it has no value apart from what it can do for us. When we translate "serve," we imply that nature/creation can be an end in itself, apart from our use of it, that we can love and serve nature as an end in itself. Perhaps most importantly, we can serve nature as its partner simply for what it is and for what it needs. In short, when I say my role is to "serve and protect" what God has made, I say that nature/creation can set the agenda of my action, that I can act *with* it, on its behalf, rather than *on* it, because of my determined needs. Let us no longer speak of ourselves as the stewards of creation. Let us say rather that we are partners with creation, a creation freely wild, as Annie Dillard says it, created by a God who loves pizzazz!

This seemingly small change in our speech can begin a new way of living in and with the creation of God. We are what we speak, since we swim in language. We desperately need a new way of speaking about creation. By replacing "till" with "serve" and "steward" with "partner," we announce our intentions to live differently with God's earth. And we proclaim our intentions to preach differently about our role in and responsibility for God's good creation. Sermons that call for our service and partnering with creation can begin the long road we face to love the earth, and by so loving love more deeply all those creatures that share it with us.

SERMON

"Conversion"

Jared Diamond in his extraordinary book of 2005, *Collapse*, says the world is faced with twelve environmental problems. These include deforestation, the loss of soils, the loss of fresh water, and the population explosion. We must solve all of them, he says, since each one alone could be our undoing. And because we continue currently along a non-sustainable course, "the world's environmental problems will get resolved, in one way or another, within the lifetimes of the children and young adults alive today."[12] What he means by one way or another

12. Jared Diamond, *Collapse*, 498.

is very unsettling; we will either solve these problems in the next fifty years, or they will plague us with frightening and unimaginable changes in our society.

Well, since I am now nearly 65 years old, these are not my problems; my children and certainly my grandchildren will need to wrestle with them. But wait. If the problems need solving in the next fifty years, I too must think about my engagement in their solution. After all, it is my generation that has added immeasurably to these vast dilemmas. What about yours? What about you?

Let's get some ground rules clear. First, let's stop arguing about whether or not we actually have these problems. There are literally thousands of books, articles, and websites that make it plain that we face extraordinary environmental difficulties. We do face problems. Second, we can do something about them; it is not too late. We Christians must be heard from as we face these monumental difficulties. Third, we Christians have crucial resources from which to draw in our Bible. In fact, a return to the scriptures is absolutely necessary if we are to begin to solve these problems. But the scriptures must be heard in fresh ways. There really is no need to turn to other spiritualities—Native American, Far Eastern, or others—to discover what we need. Our Bible is a very rich resource. Fourth, we cannot wait for science to save us or for technology to pull us out of the fire, the literal fire of rising temperatures. While science and technology will be crucially important in the besting of these problems, they alone will not be enough. Indeed, they never have been enough.

What we Christians need first is what we always have need of: conversion. We need desperately to change our ways of speaking about ourselves and nature. And if we can change our ways of speaking, we can then change our ways of acting. We swim in language; how we talk affects profoundly what we believe and how we act. But note: our conversion must be in the right order; our hearts must change before our actions can change. So, let's begin. Are you ready for a conversion?

We have long heard of Genesis 1:26–28 where God creates us in God's own image and grants us dominion over fish and bird and wild and domesticated creatures. God even bids us to "subdue" them, using a verb that can be translated "stomp on" in a military victory. Unfortunately, in too many of our interactions with God's good earth we have done precisely that: we have dominated and we have subdued, using nature for our playground, our shooting gallery, our sand pile, our kiddy pool of resources. Even though we know that our dominion is only to be exercised in the image of God, that we are to act only as God would act, the fact is we plainly have not done so. We have acted only as we want to act;

we have used creation for our ends alone, assuming that our dominion is a God-given right, and that nature is ours to do with as we please. We are stewards, we say, but in fact we act as masters without check, out of control.

We need conversion. We need new language, a new way of seeing. Again we turn to the Bible, this time to Genesis 2:15, another story of our creation. Here we are made and placed in the garden of God. What we are to do in relation to this garden can be the beginning of our conversion. Are you ready?

The translations of this verse have not helped us on the road to our needed conversion, because the translators needed conversion, too! They have read the crucial verb "dress" or "till" or "cultivate," assuming that is our primary role in creation: to act upon it, to shape it, to mold it for our own ends. But the basic meaning of this verb is "to serve," and from that verb we derive the nouns "servant" and "slave." We are not primarily called upon to act on the garden; we are called to serve the garden, to partner with it. And the second verb in the sentence adds to that meaning; we are to "protect" what we have been called to serve. So, let's now read Gen 2:15 like this: "And so YHWH God took the *'adam* and put it in the garden to serve it and to protect it." And thus our conversion may begin.

Let us put aside forever the language of tilling and cultivating and replace it with service. Let us reject the language of "steward" and use "partner" instead. With this new language we will announce to the world, and to ourselves, that creation is not for us a means to our ends alone. God's creation has its own intrinsic value and was not made for us to use in any way we can or desire. We are merely a part of that vast creation, an important part to be sure, but only a part nonetheless.

And with this new language we will gain something we twenty-first-century Christians so desperately need, a measure of humility. Finally we will say that the world does not revolve around us and our needs but revolves around God and God's desires for the wholeness and justice and community of all of God's earth and its creatures. We need this kind of conversion and we need it now. Jared Diamond says we have fifty years to be converted, though later estimates suggest that he is perhaps too generous. Nonetheless, let us begin today to speak differently, and then let us begin to act differently. The life and future of all God's creatures, the fullness of God's good earth, those creatures and that earth loved and redeemed by Jesus Christ, depend in part on you and me and on our conversion. Shall we begin our conversion today, now? The way is hard and the obstacles are mountainous. But we hold to one sure truth: with God all things, even this crucial conversion, all things are possible.

2

"The Whole Earth Is Mine"

Creation and the Psalms

Certainly human praise to God means more to God than the clatter of hail on tin roofs or the clapping of the musically inclined leaves of the aspen trees! Perhaps, but not as much as human beings would like to think.

—TERENCE FRETHEIM

WE CONCLUDED OUR SERMON in the last chapter with a cry for conversion toward a new way of understanding our human relationships to the non-human created world. A key element of that conversion was humility, based on the conviction that we humans are only a part of the immense world created and loved by the creator God. In this chapter on the Psalms and creation these twin themes of conversion and humility will be reinforced and expanded as we look more closely at the ways in which nature itself is said to praise God.

It may seem peculiar to focus attention on texts that announce the praise of God from non-human nature. After all, there are texts enough that emphasize human praise of God. Much could be said, and has been said, about Psalms 8, 33, 104, and 147, among other hymns of praise, as models of human praise of God.[1] Is not God "enthroned on the praises of Israel" (Ps 22:3)? What can we learn from those places in the Hebrew Bible where God is offered continuous praise by "hail and leaves"? What we may learn, and desperately need to learn, is that the world around us is alive with God and is in its own ways indicative of God, pointing to God and God's unique presence.

By making these claims for the praise of God by non-human nature, the Bible does not imply either a pantheism, wherein God is in everything, nor a vitalism, whereby non-human nature is somehow uniquely alive. The Bible is intent on separating God from all created things. When Psalm 24 calls worshipers to "lift their eyes to the hills" to find help, it makes it quite clear that help is not to be found in the hills, however ancient and powerful and permanent they may be, but in the God who made the hills, and who is more ancient, powerful and permanent than any hill. Still, this truth of the separation of God from God's creation has too often had the effect of denaturalizing God, that is removing God from the realities of nature and world to the point that God has no immediate role in nature at all.[2] Or it has served to disenchant nature, that is making nature out to be little more than inanimate stuff, disconnected from God and humans, valued only by their possible utility for the latter and created only for that reason by the former.

By focusing attention on the praise of God by non-human nature we humans can see that nature quite literally speaks of God, points to God, and has an important relationship to God quite apart from us. In fact, nature is alive to God and is acted upon by God, and because of that fact we are not alone in our praises. Two Psalms make these points beautifully.

Psalm 19:1–4

The skies are writing the glory of God,
  and heavens' vault narrates the work of God's hands.

---

1. Standard commentaries on the Psalms include: *The Word Biblical Commentary*, vols 19, 20, 21, Craigie, Tate, Allen; Weiser, *Psalms*; Mayes, *Psalms*. Four more specialized studies are worthy of note: Brueggemann, *The Message of the Psalms*; Holiday, *The Psalms Through Three Thousand Years*; Van Doren and Samuel, *The Book of Praise*; Alter, *The Book of Psalms*.

2. A valuable meditation on the theme of the separation of God from the natural world is McGrath, *The Reenchantment of Nature*.

> Day bubbles forth speech to day,
>> and night proclaims knowledge to night;
> Without speech, without words—
>> their voice is not heard.
> Still, their lines stretch throughout the earth,
>> their words to the world's ends!

This memorable Psalm is replete with metaphors concerning the ways that nature shouts God's praise, and many a beautiful wall poster of snow-capped mountain or burbling stream uses its language to say that we humans need to see in nature the glory of God. Notwithstanding the dangers noted above about entangling God and nature (why is God more evident in the cool highlands of Colorado than on the flat iron furnace of Texas?), a more significant problem needs mentioning. This part of the Psalm is not about us at all. This is a conversation between God and God's inanimate creation, and because this conversation uses no words or speech, we cannot even overhear what is being said! We can only look at the sky, both by day and by night, and appreciate that what we are seeing is far more than any description that science can provide. The New Mexican azure sky, studded with white puffs of cloud, is not merely a collection of certain levels of water vapor found in certain layers of measurable ion-dotted atmosphere. What is happening is a silent conversation, both written and spoken[3] between sky/vault[4] and God. The subject of that conversation is the glory of God, and the sky is persistent in its announcement of that glory twenty-four hours a day, seven days a week, in rain or snow, in sun or cloud. It may be helpful for us humans to try to listen in on the conversation, silent though it may be, but what is being "said" is glory, glory, glory. Perhaps in the same way that God puts the bow in the clouds to remind *God* of the promise never again to destroy the earth (Gen 9:15–16), so the sky, itself created by God, performs its created function by continually hymning the glory of God. The bow is not for us, and neither are the sky's cries of glory directly for us. We can observe

---

3. The verb usually translated "telling" in vs 1 is more literally derived from the verb "to write," and the noun based on the root is the word "book."

4. The Hebrew *shamayim* is regularly translated as "heavens," but its literal meaning is "sky." And in Gen 1, and elsewhere, it is "sky" that God uses as the vault or dome to divide the upper from the lower waters in creation.

and wonder, but what we can best learn is that like the sky we can add our praise of God's glory, too.

And this rather general and silent praise calls forth more specific and louder praise of God in Ps 148.

> (1)Hallelujah!
> Praise YHWH from the sky!
> Hallelujah from the heights!
> (2)Hallelujah, all God's messengers!
> Hallelujah, all God's armies!
> (3)Hallelujah, sun and moon!
> Hallelujah, all shining stars!
> (4)Hallelujah, highest sky,
> Waters above the sky!
> (5)Praise the name of YHWH!

"Hallelujah" is two Hebrew words: the plural command form "praise" and the shortened form of the Hebrew name for God, YHWH. Unlike Psalm 19, where the sky is simply said to be writing and narrating the glory of God, Psalm 148 commands that that sky, and all the created objects in it, praise their maker. Ringing changes on Gen 1, the psalmist urges that those things created in the first sky all are to praise God. It is not the sky itself that is commanded to praise but those objects found in the sky: messengers (sometimes translated "angels"), armies (sometimes translated "hosts"), sun, moon, stars, the sky above the sky ("highest sky"), and the waters above that sky, those waters pushed back in Genesis 1:6–8 by the creation of sky/vault. All these are bid to praise!

It is no accident that each of these sky objects has been seen in other cultures surrounding Israel as gods in themselves: heavenly beings ("angels"), divine armies, sun, moon, stars. But this psalmist will have none of that; these all are creatures of the one creator whose roles in the universe are to sound forth the praise of their maker. This command is made clear in the second half of vs 5 in a clause beginning with the Hebrew *ki*, "because." "Because God commanded, and they were created." These divine creations are in no doubt about three things: they are created things, YHWH is their creator, and they are created primarily to praise YHWH. Again, we humans have much to learn from these non-human creations; those three things they know we too need to know.

Now that all sky creations are commanded to praise YHWH, the psalmist announces their eternal natures and fixed realities in verse 6. "YHWH made them stand for ever and ever; YHWH gave a command that cannot pass away" (or "YHWH fixed a boundary that cannot be passed"). Whichever translation one chooses (either is possible), the sky creations are eternal realities that will grace the sky in the unchanging forms of their creation forever.

Now the psalmist turns to the earth.

> (7)Praise YHWH from the earth,
> Sea monsters and all deeps!
> (8) Fire and hail, snow and frost,
> storm wind fulfilling God's word!
> (9) Mountains and all hills,
> fruit trees and all cedars!
> (10) Wild and domesticated animals,
> crawling creatures and flying birds!

Again with memories of Genesis 1 sounding clearly, the psalmist commands the praise of God from all those creatures created on and under the earth: sea monsters (Gen 1:21), deeps (the vast cosmic seas of Gen 1:2), fire, hail, snow, frost, storm, mountains low and high, all trees, all animals, all birds. The chorus of praise is hot and cold, blustery, cawing and barking and lowing and whirring, massively silent and fruitfully rustling. Such cacaphonous praise is nearly unimaginable, profoundly deafening and deafeningly quiet at the same time. The universe is alive with the praise of God! But too often, as Elizabeth Barrett Browning observes, "the rest sit round it and pluck blackberries," though "every common bush (is) afire with God."

Here again we humans are reminded that when we praise God we are joining our voices to the silent and vocal praise of God that resounds from nature always and everywhere. To witness such praise, and to join such praise, is to see ourselves differently, not as God's unique praise chorus but as those who are part of the chorus lifted to God, the creator of it all. When we see the non-human world like this, we can begin our conversion to a new relationship with it. No longer is it merely our playground, a backdrop in front of which the human drama is played out. We can see ourselves as part of the immense drama of God's vast cosmos, all created to praise the maker, all designed to announce, each according to its own nature, the richness of God's love and care. We cannot truly love what we do not fully respect, what we do not see as a partner in the praise of God. In short, we humans need to re-enchant the nature around us. We simply must learn to speak differently about non-human nature. It is not merely our zoo, our photographic opportunities, our romantic and scenic getaways, our playscapes for boats, planes, and two-, three- and four-wheelers. Non-human nature is finally not ours at all. Psalm 24:1 needs to be emblazoned in our hearts: "The earth and everything in it belongs to YHWH." And we could also add to that memory Psalm 50:9-11, where God announces:

> I will not accept a bull from your household,
>> nor goats from your pens,
> because all the wild animals of the forest are mine,
>> domesticated animals on a thousand hills.
> I know every mountain bird,
>> and everything that moves in the field belongs to me.

But we need to return to Ps 148 to complete its important teachings for us. After the psalmist calls for the praise of everything created by God in the sky and on and under the earth, finally we humans are included in the command to praise. But the ways in which the humans are enumerated is worthy of note.

> (11) Kings of the earth and all peoples,
>> princes and all earthly leaders!
> (12) Young men and women alike,
>> old along with young!

It is a peculiar way to demonstrate the comprehensiveness of the command for human praise. It is hierarchically correct to begin the human catalogue with "kings," those leaders of the world who stand above the common folk in all things. And to pair kings with "princes and all earthly leaders" is to be expected. But what is surprising is the inclusion of the quite generic "all peoples." When it comes to the praise of God, the psalmist implies that hierarchies fall away, because all are equal at last in the command to praise the creator. And verse 12 adds to that claim, since neither age nor gender is an impediment to praise; young and old, women and men are all included in the praise chorus.

And now what a chorus we see! Soprano, quavery and pure; alto, deep and guttural; tenor, lyric and dramatic; bass, frog-like and profound; all in the human section, while the non-human adds its multitudinous growls, buzzings, cackles, and whistles. Only the creator could appreciate the cacophonous sounds that rise and descend from such a choir. However, especially the human members of the choir must learn the crucial contributions of the non-human members, for without them we know that the choir is not complete, as the next verse makes plain.

> (13) Let them praise the name of YHWH,
>> for God's name alone is exalted,
>> God's glory above earth and sky!

The "them" of the first line is fully inclusive of all created things mentioned in the remainder of the Psalm. Unless all praise the name of YHWH, that name alone cannot be fully and appropriately exalted, God's glory not fully and appropriately witnessed to as constitutive of the one who creates and rules over all those created and loved.

Whenever the name of YHWH is lifted in praise, any reader of the Hebrew Bible necessarily harkens back to the scene in the narrative traditions of Israel where YHWH is most memorably defined—Exodus 34:6–7. Moses' request to see the glory of God (33:18) is both denied, as YHWH reveals only God's "back" ("train"? "wake"?), yet also affirmed as several memorable descriptive nouns and adjectives reveal the purpose and work of YHWH.

> (6) YHWH passed in front of Moses' face and proclaimed,
>> "YHWH, YHWH, a God compassionate and gracious,
>> slow to anger, filled with unbreakable love and faithfulness,
> (7) keeping unbreakable love for thousands,
> bearing iniquity, and transgression, and sin,
>> but not simply clearing the guilty,
>> visiting the iniquity of the ancestors on the children,
>> and on the children's children,
>> to the third and the fourth generation."

It is this YHWH, the righteous and compassionate judge, whose glory and name are commanded to be praised by all of God's creations. With YHWH's unbreakable love, to be contrasted with the broken tablets of human sin, as the very hallmark of who YHWH is, the call to praise must be answered by all those creatures who know they are created by this God, and must be answered even by those creatures who do not "know" that, at least in any way that we humans can "know."

Ps 148 ends on what sounds on the surface to be a completely human note.

> (14) God has lifted up a horn for God's people,
>> a praise song for all God's faithful ones,
>> for the people of Israel who are close to God.
>> Hallelujah!

If the nouns of these three lines are synonymous, then "God's people," "God's faithful ones," and "the people of Israel" all refer to human beings. However, in the context of this extraordinarily comprehensive psalm, is it not possible that "God's faithful ones" should include all those created creatures mentioned throughout the poem? Are not trees and wind and beasts all the faithful ones of God in that they are commanded to give praise to their maker? Hence, both people and non-human creatures make up the choir of praise from the beginning of the psalm to its end.

Thus again our conversion toward nature and our humility in the face of nature are reaffirmed in this remarkable poem. We can now see that the skies indeed write and narrate the glory of God, that the mountains and the sea monsters sound forth God's praise, that the sun and the moon in their silent courses praise the God of sky and earth. A twentieth-century hymn nicely captures the riches of the diverse chorus of praise, "Earth and all Stars," words by Herbert F. Brokering, music by David N. Johnson, both from 1968. In this stirring hymn, earth and all stars, hail, wind, rain, flowers, and trees all "sing to the Lord a new song." And in the last verse, "daughter and son, loud praying members" are added to the singers. Yet, in the light of the ancient Psalm 148, the "new" song of the hymn is not new at all. It is just that in our new day of environmental degradation, we humans need to see anew the full chorus of praise that God, the creator, has called forth from the very beginning of creation.

SERMON

"Earth and All Stars"

I have sung in choirs all my life: children's choirs, youth choirs, and adult choirs of professional quality and less than professional quality. Nothing thrills me more than to sing with a choir and an orchestra some great piece of classical music: the Brahms or Mozart or Verdi requiems, Mendelssohn's "Elijah," Vaughn Williams' "Hodie," or Handel's "Messiah." I get goose bumps just remembering my experiences in these choirs.

I imagine I was soprano or alto before my male voice set in, and then I traversed with my vocal cords down the octaves from high watery tenor to now something like a bass-baritone. For me, only the day of my wedding, and the days of the births of our two children, can match the joy and excitement I have felt singing in a choir. I love solos, and have sung many of them, but in the long run I love a choir more.

But after reading and pondering Psalm 148, I have discovered that my understanding of choir is too small. Standing and singing praise to God in brilliant human music is marvelous indeed, but it is too narrow a way of thinking about choirs. It turns out that my human choir of praise is not only too small, not only very late on the scene of praise, but it is finally too exclusive in its membership. We need sopranos, altos, tenors, and basses, all right, but we also need lions, and tigers, and bears, oh my! And we need trees and grass and mountains. And we need sun, moon, and stars. And how about a bug or two?

But wait, you say. You can't find a bear that reads music, nor a mountain that can carry a tune, not to mention those awful little bugs! Just what sort of choir do you have in mind? What sort of chorus might this be, with its screeches and growls and clatterings, ill-matched with four-part harmonies and blended human voices? Well, I am glad you asked, because I will tell you just what sort of choir this one is. It is God's universal choir of praise, and it turns out that I may need the growls and screeches in this choir far more than they need my bass-baritone. And just why might that be?

Psalm 148 commands the praise of God literally from all the things created by that God. The list is fully comprehensive. First, the sky is addressed and commanded that all those created objects found in the sky are to praise YHWH:

divine messengers, the heavenly armies, sun and moon, all the stars, even the sky above the sky and its water, the source of our refreshing rains. They are to praise God, because God commanded their creation and fixed them for all eternity as signs of God's power and permanence. Second, the creations connected to earth are commanded to join the praise of God: the vast oceans and their mysterious sea monsters, fire and hail, snow and frost and hurricane wind. Then are added mountains, trees, and the rich diversity of animals, both wild and domesticated. The vast chorus assembles and howls and whispers and silently offers its praise.

Then we humans are asked to join, young and old, men and women, king and pauper, add our human sounds to the roars and silences of the innumerable array. "Let them praise the name of YHWH, for only YHWH's name is exalted, only YHWH's glory overreaches both earth and sky."

Is this chaotic choir of praise finally just a fanciful and nonsensical picture of my fevered imagination? Is it just the tree-hugger in my environmental soul that conjures this cacophonous chorus of bear and bass, tenor and titmouse, alto and aardvark, soprano and swordfish? Not quite, I do not think, though I will admit to a fair amount of tree-hugging in my life. After all, the psalmist who sang 148 beat me to it. That old poet caught the truth of our need to join the great and vast chorus of praise to the creator God. And unless sky and earth, and all that is in them, are in the chorus, the full harmonies of praise are impossible to create. What we need, too, are different ears in our evaluation of the members of the choir. Barks and growls and buzzes are as important in the chorus as altos and basses, and until I know that, until I believe that, our choir will be incomplete and our relationships to our fellow creatures necessarily broken.

So let's change the words of our hymn just slightly.

> Earth and all stars, loud rushing planets,
> Sing to the Lord an old song!

It is the old song of Ps 148. It is the old song of praise to God. It is the old song that unites all of God's creation into one chorus and makes clear and true the work that Jesus Christ came to do. The famous John 3:16 says it best: "God so loved the cosmos, all that is, that God gave the only son, so that everyone who believes in him may not die but may have an undying life."

The chorus of praise is incomplete until all the creation of God is seen as member. And until we can see that, really see that vast chorus, we can never love what it is that God loves. And what we cannot love we cannot care for. And what we cannot care for, we can easily forget. A human choir's four-part harmony is sweet and greatly to be praised, but four parts are not enough, have never been enough. I must welcome the bears and the oleanders and the hills into the choir of praise if I can ever see myself as their partner on the earth. Today, now, this minute, as we face environmental challenges too numerous to list and too scary to contemplate, we first must add to the choir of praise.

So, look at the choir. Are the lions among the tenors? Are the squirrels skittering around the sopranos? Do palm trees dot the ranks of the altos? Are the basses blessed with lemurs? If not, the choir is not full, and the praise of God is weak, short-changed, finally out of tune. Yes, I love to sing in a choir, but it is this new, vast, heterogeneous choir I want now to join. We all need to join this new choir. Are you ready to sing? Well, God is past ready to hear.

3

"Where Were You?"

Creation and the Book of Job

Anyway, maybe there weren't any solutions. Human society, they claimed,
was a sort of monster, its main by-products being corpses and rubble. It never
learned, it made the same cretinous mistakes over and over, trading short-term
gain for long-term pain. It was like a giant slug eating its way relentlessly
through all the other bioforms on the planet, grinding up life on earth and
[evacuating] it out the backside in the form of pieces of manufactured and
soon-to-be-obsolete plastic junk.

—MARGARET ATWOOD

MARGARET ATWOOD'S *ORYX AND CRAKE*,[1] that grim little piece of an
apocalyptic novel, announces again the desperate need we all have for
new ways of thinking about the environment and our relationships to
it. In this regard, there is no more important piece of the Bible than the
Book of Job. I have spent nearly my entire scholarly life wrestling with the
complexities of this book (nearly 40 years), yet my writing and reflect-
ing on it did not yield its significance for matters ecological until I read

1. Atwood, *Oryx and Crake*.

the work of Norman Habel and a small book of Bill McKibben.[2] Through their eyes, focused squarely on the environment, Job's unforgettable story becomes absolutely crucial as a guide to our needed new thinking about the creation.

On the surface, the story of Job is quite simple. A superbly righteous man (1:1) is chosen by God for a test to see whether or not he loves and serves God for God's own sake or for the good things he can receive from God. In the first two chapters, Job appears to prove the Satan wrong, and God right, when he, Job, refuses to curse God even when, for no apparent reason, he loses everything he formerly prized: his home, family, goods, and finally health and reputation.

But chapter 3 begins a long and increasingly rancorous debate concerning the reasons for Job's astounding descent to the ash-heap. His three friends, Eliphaz, Bildad, and Zophar, say in as many ways as their overactive imaginations can conjure, that Job must have sinned to end up in his present condition. They are convinced of this, because they know that the world is centrally based on the principle that good behavior receives rich reward while bad behavior receives appropriate punishment from a God who is always in the business of evening up the scores of human life. Job's current position among the orange peels and fish bones of the town dump are proof positive that he has done well-nigh unimaginable evil at some time in his life. He is in desperate need of immediate confession and repentance. Examples of these beliefs of the friends are found throughout their speeches (4:6–11, Eliphaz; 8:2–7, Bildad; 11:2–6, Zophar; among many others).

Job responds to these cruel demands by direct rejections of the friends' claims (6:14–30; 12:2–3; 16:2–5; 19:2–6 as representative examples), and by furious indictments of God, the author of this feast of horrors (6:4; 9:22–24; 16:7–17; 19:7–22). Job and his friends agree on one thing; God does reward the righteous and punish the wicked. However, the friends believe that that nostrum is working precisely in the case of Job, while Job is convinced that God has made some sort of mistake this time, since Job has done nothing to deserve his fate (see, for example, 7:12, where Job accuses God of confusing him with the great Canaanite sea monster Yam,

---

2. Habel, *The Book of Job,* and two of his more recent articles: "Earth First: Inverse Cosmology in Job," and "'Is the Wild Ox Willing to Serve You?' Challenging the Mandate to Dominate,"; Bill McKibben, *The Comforting Whirlwind.*

muzzling him rather than the beast of the sea who needs muzzling to keep him under God's control).

The friends and Job verbally wrestle back and forth to a crescendo of invective and satiric assault for twenty-seven chapters, after which another furious friend, Elihu, pours out his own invective on Job for six more. By most ancient comparisons, the book of Job is not a long one, but reading this debate straight through can be an exhausting and dispiriting experience. Along with Job, the reader cries out, "if only I had someone to hear me! Let Shaddai answer me!" (31:35). We, like Job, are desperate for a word from God. And finally God appears.

But the two speeches of the Almighty may not be quite what Job or we expected. Indeed, the speeches of God have called forth a staggering array of diverse commentary. Some have said that God's simple appearance to Job is enough to cause Job's supposed "repentance" in 42:6; God's presence is sufficient in and of itself to end the drama happily.[3] Yet, this finally will not do. God does in fact *speak* to Job at some considerable length and in quite lovely and powerful poetry. Surely, God's "answer" to Job is more than God's appearance to him. Others have said that God's speeches quite simply put Job in his human place, and tell him to shut up and to stop questioning the ways of God that he can never hope to understand.[4] There is truth in this reading, but it is only a partial truth. "Shut up, little twit," seems a poor response to the agonized questions of Job, however grand the poetic expression may be!

Still others note that God refuses to address directly the questions posed by Job, and by the friends. The central question is the justice of the universe, as that justice has been construed by those human beings. In that reading, God's speeches are long non sequiturs, pushing the discussion in ways it had not even hinted at going. Job demands justice and God speaks of ostriches![5] Read like that, it does seem monumentally beside the point. But this implies that the composer of the God speeches had an

3. See, for example, Terrien, "The Book of Job," 901, who says, "The vision of God is enough."

4. See, for example, Driver and Gray, *The Book of Job*, 325, who say, "The main body of (God's) speech is designed to bring out the immensity of Job's ignorance and the greatness of God's knowledge and His beneficent use of it."

5. So, for example, R.N. Carstensen, *Job: Defense of Honor*, or McKenzie, "The Purpose of the Yahweh Speeches in the Book of Job," 436, who says the speeches are "like waving a rattle before a crying infant, to distract him from his hunger."

agenda quite other than the composer of the dialogue. This is, of course, possible, given the composite nature of this complex text, but is there no way to connect what God is saying to Job with what Job has been saying to and about God?

An environmental reading connects the God speeches to the remainder of the book. The opening divine speech (38–39) makes one fact quite clear, a fact I have been presenting as central to the Bible's presentations of human-nature relationships. In this long first speech God paints a picture of a world without human beings, yet at the same time a world cared for by God! Chapter 38:25–27 states this quite explicitly:

> (25) Who has cut a channel for the rain,
> a way for the sound of thunder,
> (26) to bring rain on a land without people,
> a wilderness where no human exists,
> (27) to satisfy a place of wasted desolation,
> to make the ground sprout grass?

In this representative passage of God's deep meteorological and cosmic concerns (38:4–38), the ongoing actions of wind and rain and storm and ice and cloud are performed without human concern of any kind. God cuts rain channels and thunder roads sometimes in order to bring the rain onto places devoid of human life, indeed onto blasted, uninhabited wilderness places, places that then burst into verdant life. And no one, save God, sees this drama take place! McKibben makes the point of this wonder very clear: "[W]hat stronger way could there be to make the point, what more overpowering fact to rebut the notion that we are forever at the center of all affairs. The first meaning, I think, of God's speech to Job is that we are a part of the whole order of creation—simply a part."[6] So again, as we saw in Genesis and in the Psalms, the biblical record reminds us of this crucial fact; we are not finally all there is in God's created world.

But there is more. I said above that some readers of these speeches have concluded that their basic function is to humble Job, to put him in his place, to remind him that he is only human. This, as I said, is partly true. Surely, Job is arrogant, and is in need of a corrective interview by the God who is far more than he imagined. But the tone of the speech is not merely furious or defensive or obnoxious. God does not only say, "Shut

---

6. Mckibben, *The Comforting*, 37.

up!" God also says, "Open your eyes, Job. The world around you, of which you are a part, is wild and free and gritty and bloody." McKibben says it like this:

> Job complains that the world makes no sense and God shows him the little vultures drinking blood (39:30). That is [God's] answer— little vultures drinking blood. We are beyond categories here, and into the rich, tough, gristly fabric of life.[7]

And he goes on: "That sense of ebullient, shivery wildness runs throughout this whole poem—the 'foolish' ostrich redeemed by her pure speed, her pure laughing speed (39:13–18). This is not the tame and citified vision of the lion lying down with the lamb—it is a rapacious, tough, deadly, amoral, glorious wildness."[8] God says to Job, who claims to know and understand far more than he does, and God says to us, who claim to stand in the very center of all things, that "it is not a storybook that we were born into, but a rich and complicated novel without any conclusion. Every page of this novel speaks of delight—not rational, painless, comfortable, easy pleasure, but delight."[9]

God does not only take Job down a peg or two. God shows him the rich panoply of heaven and earth and calls him to joy, bids him to rejoice in it. God's tone is as much invitational as it is harsh, as much loving call as it is enumeration of Job's shortcomings. Job and we need very much to hear God fully.

But Job does not. His first response to God reveals clearly that he hears only harshness and mockery. I have suggested elsewhere[10] that Job's response to this first speech of God is testy, an angry acquiescence to a divine bully.

(4) Look! I am accursed (or trifling)! How can I answer you?
   I lay my hand on my mouth.
(5) Once I have spoken, but I no longer answer,
   twice, but no more.

Job has only heard God say, "Shut up," and he shuts up. He vows to stop responding, laying his hand on his mouth in the way that Israelites have

---

7. M McKibben, *The Comforting*, 55.

8. Mckibben, *The Comforting*, 57.

9. McKibben, *The Comforting*, 57.

10. Holbert, *Preaching Job*, 129–32.

long done when faced with a superior power (see 21:5; 29:9; Mic 7:16). But if I am right that God is doing more than silencing Job, such a response from him will not do. And it does not, for there is another speech from God.

The second divine speech begins in exactly the same way that the first begins. The verses at 38:2 and 40:7 are identical. But the verse that follows, 40:8, is significantly different.

> Will you really suppress/annul my judgment,
>> condemn me so that you may be justified?

This divine question proves that God has been listening to the dialogue after all, and demonstrates by implication that the first speech of God was not beside the point at all. God really was answering Job in the first speech, even though Job heard no answer to his perceived problem. But now Job's silent answer to God's question of 40:8 is surely "yes." Job has throughout his long speeches fought to suppress or annul God's judgment of him ("to put God in the wrong," as the NRSV has it). Job, like his friends, assumes throughout that God has been judging him, has dropped him onto the rubbish heap, and has done so by mistake or perhaps for some hidden and sinister purpose (so 10:12–13). As a result, Job has in fact condemned God (so 9:22–24), thinking that in the zero sum game of the universe, if Job is justified, then God must be condemned.

Chapter 40:9–14 says to Job that Job's construal of the universe is completely false. Though some commentators read these verses as a continuation of the harsh tone of God that they heard in the first speech, baiting Job to try to be like God, laughing at his complete failure to be able to do so, I hear the speech differently. I think that God delivers these lines with a twinkle in the eye, rather than a snarl on the lip. God invites Job to do precisely what God does not do! Go ahead, Job, says God; "tread down the wicked, hide them in the dust together, tie them up in some hidden place." Do all that, says God, and I will admit that your right hand has given you the victory that you seem to imagine you need. Go ahead! I'll watch, says God. Then, God stands aside and watches, and there is a pause in the action between 40:14 and 40:15. Because, obviously, Job cannot do those things that he assumes God does for the simple fact that God does not do those things either! God does not tread down the wicked, stomp them into the dust, tie them up in hidden places. The God imagined by Job and his friends simply does not exist!

Chapter 40:15 makes that certain.

> Just have a look at Behemoth,
>> which I made along with you!

Earlier translators attempted in their own rational way to domesticate this creature by translating the word Behemoth as hippopotamus, assuming that the poet was describing a known creature in the manner of the first divine speech's catalogue of animals. But the word should here be rendered "The Beast," since this is an ancient mythological creature from Canaanite texts, representing the forces of chaos overcome by the power of the great god Baal. And it is further an example of even earlier stories from the Mesopotamian valley.[11] God made chaos in the same way, and even perhaps at the same time, that God made Job. Again, Job is put in his proper place in the creation, but more, God reveals that "chaos and evil are part of the world,[12] "and are not dealt with by God's immediate destruction. YHWH does not destroy Behemoth, nor Leviathan (also a creature of chaos made by God and described in chapter 41), in order that Job may live free in a perfectly ordered and moral world. The existence of Behemoth and Leviathan, and their creation by YHWH, suggest that the cosmos is far messier than Job and his friends had imagined.

And now that Job has been decentered by God and has had his understanding of the universe and God thoroughly reshaped, Job's famous final speech can be better understood. Chapter 42:5–6 is the key.

> (5) By the ear's hearing I had heard of you,
>> but now my eyes see you.

Job knew only what the friends knew about God, namely what he had been taught but not experienced. Now he has experienced God and has discovered that the God of hearsay is no God at all, and that the conclusions he drew from that hearsay need a complete rejection and reformulation.

> (6) Therefore I retract,
>> and I am sorry on dust and ashes.

11. Pope, *Job*, 320.
12. Habel, *Job*, 564.

This is a difficult verse, and it has been read in numerous ways. My reading depends heavily on my expectations of what I think Job must now do in the face of his meeting with YHWH. He must first "retract"[13] those dreadful things he said about God, things now made absurd in the light of his new knowledge of God. (It needs to be said forcefully that the NRSV's translation "I despise myself" is plainly impossible grammatically and leaves a thoroughly false impression of Job's meaning.) And in the second line, Job does not repent in any traditional religious sense, but rather "changes his mind" (so Ex 32:12, 14; Gen 6:6), thereby forsaking his posture of lamentation and fury on his ash heap. By so speaking Job resolves to give up his adversarial stance with God in order to move toward a reconciliation with the God he now knows is not his enemy but his fellow struggler with chaos.

Job becomes a new person after his encounter with God, but note something very important about the encounter. "When God spoke to Job, [God] did not reveal [Godself]; [God] revealed [God's] works."[14] That is, God's works, God's trees and lions and "monsters," need to be seen and cherished and protected quite apart from our constant emphasis on *our* search for God. As I have said, it is quite true for the Bible that God is not to be confused with God's works, lest we worship the creation rather than the creator. But if we neglect the creation as a mere backdrop to our human behaviors, we deny what God revealed to Job. We are a part of that creation; our proper stance in relationship to it is humility; that creation has its own intrinsic value to God quite apart from us; that God has created a wilder and freer creation than our tiny orthodoxies have traditionally allowed.

Let me give Bill McKibben the last lyrical word concerning what we must learn from the poet of Job.

> We need to stop thinking so much in terms of our "environment." An environment is a human creation: the home environment, the office environment. It counts—we need clean air and clean water, of course. But our environment is only a small part of something much larger. A planet, filled with the vast order of creation. It is a buzzing, weird, stoic, abundant, reckless, haunting, painful, per-

13. The Hebrew verb, *m's*, always takes a direct object, except here. Pope, *Job*, 348, assumes that the object is clearly implied, though not stated; it is "my words." My reading "retract" makes a similar point.

14. Mckibben, *The Comforting*, 83.

fect planet. All of it matters, all of it is glorious. And all of it can speak to us in the deepest and most satisfying ways, if only we will let it.[15]

SERMON

Answer to Job

How can you answer a man like Job? Just listen to his questions! "Why is light given to a man whose way is hidden from him?" "Am I the monster of the sea that you muzzle me?" "God destroys righteous and wicked and laughs while they die! If it is not God, then who is it?" "How often is the lamp of the wicked really put out?" "How can you ever comfort me with these empty nothings?" I mean, how can you answer a man with questions like these?

Questions like these are bold and arrogant and presumptuous, demanding responses that no human can finally give. Oh, his friends try to answer all right; they answer at length, *ad naseum.* "You are evil, Job; that is why you are on the ash heap and why you are asking such terrible questions. Only sinners talk like you. What you need is repentance and reconciliation with the God who has justly punished you." But Job will have none of it. "I have done nothing worthy of these assaults from God, for it is of course God who is doing this. But God has blown it this time, made a mistake, messed up, gotten confused. I will keep questioning until I get satisfaction!"

And so it goes for chapter after chapter, neither side quitting, neither side giving in. "I want my justice," screams Job. "You are getting the only justice there is," shout the friends, "the harsh and true justice of God who will not abide foul sinners." Yet, these are not answers, not genuine responses. And even the questions, truth be told, are hardly real questions. They are rather accusations, because the world, as they all think they know it, is not working for Job, and he wants to know why. Obviously only God can take this mess on; only God can untangle this unholy mess; only God can cut this Gordian knot.

And God does, but not at all in the way that Job or the friends or we imagined it. First, God has got a question. "Who is this who obscures my design with empty-headed words?" In that one harsh blast God calls into question all of Job's

15. McKibben, *The Comforting*, 95.

questions. His questions, it turns out, are obscuring God's design, indicating that Job has not the foggiest notion of that design, and more the questions are uttered out of an empty brain. In short, Job's questions are not the right questions at all to God.

Job needs all manner of revelation to get him on the right track. We need all manner of revelation if we are ever to ask the right questions. Job asks about his justice, his restoration, his vindication. God answers by showing Job God's works. Have a look at this, Job, shouts God, like a kid with a new toy. Rain for the desert where no one in their right mind would live. Yet, the grass comes up all the same with no human to see it or animal to eat it. It just is, just nice grass for itself, for God. How about this, Job? Lions eat without human help; vultures drink blood away from human sight. Ostriches abandon their young without sense, but when they run, they laugh uproariously as they pass everything in the race. The world is rich and rare and strange, and messy and thorny and not always safe. Do you get it, Job? Your justice is not the question; the cosmos is the question. Where you fit in the whole cosmos is the question.

But Job doesn't get it. "You win, you big bully. What do I care about lions and ostriches and useless rain? I shut up; that is what you want, so I shut up."

But God will have none of that. "Pay attention now! Do you think I have to be wrong so you can be right?" Darn tootin', says Job in so many words. "If you reward good folks and punish bad folks in the ways I have heard, then my punishment is unfair. Hence, you are wrong, and that makes me right!"

"OK, Job," says God. "If you think that is what I do—reward and punish, why don't you do it? I will stand over here, and you stomp on a few wicked people, tie them up together, and cram them into the dirt. You do that, and I will call you a mighty fine punisher. Go on. Have at it!"

Job cannot do this, and it begins to dawn on him that God does not do it either. Maybe a closer look at ostriches and lions and vultures and desert rains might do Job a world of good. Might put him in the proper place in the cosmos, might help him think about different questions. But he needs to see a different God before he can do that. So a different God shows up. And out of the divine throne room lumbers Behemoth, a nasty old creature of chaos who arches his mighty back and earthquakes occur. "Have a look at this," shouts God, with another new toy. "I made this thing just as I made you; he and you are both part of my design. You see, Job, my design is not so simple when you see Behemoth and Leviathan—that other huge thing of chaos over there—who are in the mix with you. My world is vast, but not easily captured, all-encompassing but very untidy. Any questions?"

No questions now. "My knowledge of you was flat wrong, God," says Job. "Your rain-filled wilderness and animal parade make that clear. I think I need to retract my questioning accusations and say I change my mind on this ashy dust."

So how do you answer a man like Job? You get a new view of God, a new view of the cosmos, and finally a new view of yourself. And so it is with us. If we are ever to ask the right questions, we need to know that the cosmos is not ours alone, but that we are a part of a vast and messy design, created and held together by God. And we need to see God differently, not as some mechanical monster, rewarding and punishing on some cosmic spread sheet. God needs to be free, untamed, to some extent mysterious, and definitely beyond all of our imaginings. In short, we need a Joban experience of God. Are you ready? Any questions?

4

"I Am About to Do a New Thing"

Creation and the Hebrew Prophets

There will always be pigeons in books and in museums, but these are effigies and images, dead to all hardships and to all delights. Book-pigeons cannot dive out of a cloud to make the deer run for cover, or clap their wings in thunderous applause of mast-laden woods.... For one species to mourn the death of another is a new thing under the sun. The Cro-Magnon who slew the last mammoth thought only of steaks. The sportsman who shot the last pigeon thought only of his prowess. But we, who have lost our pigeons, mourn the loss.

—ALDO LEOPOLD

I CAN HARDLY DO justice in one brief chapter to the rich commentary concerning creation to be found in the prophetic literature of Israel. This literature covers over two hundred years and encompasses many different prophetic personalities. Nevertheless, the theme of creation plays a significant role in nearly all of these prophets, and it is important that a preacher have some entrée into their ideas. As before in this book, I will focus on specific texts to provide entry points into the literature as a whole.

It is generally agreed that the oldest of the writing prophets of Israel was Amos, who served a very short ministry in and around the central shrine of the northern kingdom of Israel, Bethel, (to be distinguished from the southern kingdom Judah and its central shrine and capital Jerusalem) about the middle of the eighth century BCE. Amos' preaching revolved around one main claim: though the northerners felt comfortable in their prosperity, that prosperity and ease were constructed on the backs of the poor of the land. Amos peers deeply into the heart of Israel and finds there a godless greed, a rotten cancer that is leading it to exile and death.

But his analysis is not merely a social/political one, however much the high priest, Amaziah, interpreted his words in precisely that way (Amos 7:10–13); Amos above all was speaking theologically. His sermons made it clear that the God he came to proclaim was centrally interested in human behavior as it did or did not conform to the rigors of God's righteous demands for justice (see 5:21–24 as the classic example). Yet, what Amos provided, perhaps for the first time in human history, was an analysis of the "rich interrelatedness of social and cosmic orders."[1] That is, the God of righteous justice is at the same time the creator God of the universe.

He demonstrates this connection by his use of doxologies at crucial junctures of his sermons. Chapter 4:4–13 offers an example. Verses 4–5 begin the sermon with words laden with sarcasm as Amos mocks the call of the priests to "come to church:"

> (4) Come to Bethel—and sin!
>> Gilgal—maximize sin!
> Bring sacrifices every morning,
>> your tithes every three days,
> (5) a thank-offering of unleavened bread;
>> announce free-will offerings—advertise!
>> For so you love to do, people of Israel!

And while the people are worshipping and praising God with extravagant gifts and loud and boisterous song, that same God has been trying to speak to them through environmental disasters: famine (vs. 6), drought (vss. 7–8), agricultural disease and insect pests (vs. 9), human and ani-

---

1. Fretheim, *God and World*, 171.

mal plague (vs. 10), and cosmic conflagration in the manner of Sodom and Gomorrah (vs. 11). But their eyes are blinded by their rich offerings and their ears are diverted by the wonders of their worship; none of these events caused them to "return to God." It is crucial not to hear these verses as some sort of magical understanding of a God who blights the world in order to warn humanity that it needs to repent or else. These verses do not teach us to believe in a God who uses nature as direct warning signs of God's anger and God's power, however much certain modern believers have attempted to affirm such a view.[2] They rather announce that the social orders of human life and the cosmic orders of the larger environment are inextricably interrelated. Those of us in the twenty-first century know this fact all too well.

We know that famine in our world is the result of a deadly combination of drought, poor soil, rising temperatures due to human indifference, political greed, inequitable division of resources, poor human choices, and a host of other factors. Amos' claim that in the face of drought, "still Israel did not return to God," is a sermon to us who are able to control some of the factors that lead to famine in our world. Our return to God could engender the will to practice that control.

The fact that Amos ends his sermon of chapter 4 with a doxology, hymning the creator God, makes his point that the relationships between the social order and the cosmic order go both ways. It is a fact that the natural order is directly affected by human behaviors (see Hos 4:1–3 for another example). Moreover, God's creation impinges on human order by the simple fact that God is an ongoing creator. This is no deist God, winding the watch of the world, and disappearing into semi-retirement.

> (13) Now look! The one who forms the mountains and creates the wind,
>> narrates designs to humans,
>> making the morning darkness,
>> and walking on the high places of the earth!

2. In recent times some very public statements have been made by national religious leaders, suggesting that events have been enacted by God precisely to warn or punish persons who refuse to act in ways demanded by this same God. For example, Rev. Jerry Falwell said that "God had removed the veil of protection from the USA," allowing the terrorist attacks of 9/11/01, due directly to certain behaviors from certain Americans (abortions, homosexuality, liberal thinking, etc.). Rev. Pat Robertson, echoing Falwell, claimed that certain hurricanes were sent by God as warnings of greater disasters to come unless "mass repentance," as defined by Rev. Robertson, occurred.

YHWH, God of the armies—that's the name!

God not only forms the mountains but strolls on them, too. God not only makes the wind but each morning spreads the dawn upon the land. Those who would worship this God must be ready to reckon with a present God, an active God, a continually creating God whose righteous demands are constant, providing a measuring rod against which all human community is to be measured.

The promised future of God is described in a lyrically natural ending to Amos' prophecy (9:11–15). Though many have argued that these words have been added to the older words of Amos,[3] they make a fitting end to a series of sermons that began with a blighted environment of withered and dry pastures (1:2), made so by the lion-like roar of the word of God. But after Amos's many harsh pronouncements of that same divine word, God's will for Israel and the cosmos is found beautifully portrayed at 9:13.

> Look! The days are coming, says YHWH,
>> when the one who plows will meet the reaper,
>> and the sower of seed the treader of grapes.
> The mountains will drip wine,
>> and all the hills will be drenched in it!

Such a picture of fecundity can hardly be imagined! The reaper of the crop cannot get out of the way of the plow, so rapidly and richly will the land produce, while the grape treader will find her feet stepping on more than grapes; the next crop of grapes is already being sown! And as far as the eye can see, the mountains and the hills will be awash in wine. This is not some return to Eden; this is the restoration and rejuvenation of the blighted land, a land spoiled by the greed and exploitation of the few against the many. When justice reigns, the cosmos will be healed. Amos knew well that the creator God was in the business of far more than human justice. This God of the cosmos desires nothing less than a freshly restored universe.

And Amos' prophetic colleague, the unnamed prophet of the exile we know as Second Isaiah, writing some two hundred years after Amos in a vastly different time in the life of the people, places Amos's great vi-

---

3. Two examples among many are: James Luther Mays, *Amos*, 163–68; James M. Ward, *Amos and Isaiah*, 87–90. Ward reiterates his belief in his *Thus Says the Lord*, 212–13.

sion of creation on an even more stupendous stage. It is this prophet of Babylonian exile who offers the most extraordinary portrait of the inter-relatedness of the creator God and human behavior.

Second Isaiah's sixteen chapters of fertile language are saturated with creation imagery, but I will focus attention on the wonderful chapter 43. The context of the prophet's word is the exiled community in Babylon. That community, the survivors of the two assaults on Jerusalem in 597/587 BCE, lived in the city for some sixty years, only being released by the edict of Cyrus of Persia in 539 BCE. Because Second Isaiah mentions Cyrus directly in chapter 45:1, his words must have been written very late in the sojourn in Babylon. Chapter 43:1 nicely captures the tenor and tone of the prophecy.

> And now thus says YHWH,
>> the one who created you, Jacob,
>> the one who shaped you, Israel,
>> "Do not be afraid, because I have vindicated you.
>> I have called you by your name; you are mine!"

Note first the very clear connection between creation and redemption/vindication. YHWH is hymned as the creator and shaper of Jacob/Israel, harking back to the most ancient designations of the people, the heirs of the trickster, Jacob, whose name became Israel after his mysterious confrontation with a man at the river Jabbok in Genesis 32:22–32. YHWH "created" (*bara'*) and YHWH "shaped" (*yatsar*), each word regularly used as signs of the unique work of the creator God (see, for example, Gen 1:1; 2:7). And because God has created and shaped Israel, these exiles, many of whom have never seen their lost homeland, need no longer be afraid, because the creator has also already done the work of vindication/redemption (*ga'al*). This extraordinary work of redemption is Second Isaiah's favorite description of the work of YHWH for Israel. The verbal root, *ga'al*, and its nominal uses, comprise 15 references to God and God's work in his brief book. The meaning of this word may best be gained from its use in two other contexts.

It is a common way to express the work of God in freeing the Israelites from Egyptian bondage (Ex 6:6; 15:13; Pss 74:2; 77:16; 78:35; 106:10). And, in its more domestic meaning, it describes the responsibility of the closest next of kin to take care of female members of the family who have been widowed; this act of redemption is designed in law to ensure that the widowed member is saved from the dangers of separation from the community and its support system (the book of Ruth is a classic story example of this legal requirement: see Ruth 2:20, 3:9,12, 4:1, 3, 6, 8, 14). In these two instances, we can see that redemption/vindication means in fact freedom from bondage and freedom from exploitation and fear. Second Isaiah announces that the community in exile can embrace YHWH's redemption and is thus free from the bondage of exile and the fear of foreign exploitation. And these freedoms are rooted in the great act of the creation of Israel.

But that is not the only creative act of YHWH that ensures the certainty of the vindication of YHWH. 43:2 adds an older element:

> Whenever you pass through the waters, I am with you,
> and through the rivers, they shall not sweep you away.
> Whenever you walk with fire, you shall not be burned;
> no flame shall consume you.

The poet now reverts to the first great act of YHWH's redemption, the Exodus from Egypt. No mention of "passing through the waters" could fail to evoke the memory of that signature redemptive act of YHWH, the act that transformed Israel from the terrified slaves of Pharaoh into the people of YHWH. This is the event that grounds Israel's ongoing life as a people and offers the very reason for their unique existence and responsibilities as God's own (see especially the announcement of the first of the ten commandments both in Ex 20 and Deut 5).

But, of course, passing through the waters of the Sea of Reeds at the Exodus itself calls forth an even older memory of the creation of the world. The third act of God in creation, after the creation of light and sky, is the division of the waters under the sky in order that the dry land, the place of plant, animal, and human habitation, may appear. This movement of waters is an older prefiguring of the movement of waters at the Sea of Reeds.

And by mentioning "fire" in the second half of chapter 43:2, the prophet again reminds the exiles of their time in the wilderness with the pillar of fire that both separated them from the Egyptian armies and lighted their way through the wasteland toward their destiny at the sea. Water and fire are the two basic elements of creation, and in the hands of YHWH they have become tools for the redemption of God's chosen people. Here again, creation both precedes and interacts with the salvific and redemptive work of God. The prophet reiterates this connection later in chapter 43:14–17, saying that the "Redeemer YHWH" (vs 14) is also the "Creator YHWH" (vs 15), "who makes a way in the sea" to provide victory for the people.

Still, the great poet has one more twist to add to the creative and redemptive work of YHWH. Very surprisingly, the prophet now commands:

> (18) Do not remember the first things!
> Do not reflect on old things!
> (19) Watch! I am doing a new thing:
> it springs up! Don't you know it?
> I am surely making a road in the wilderness,
> rivers in the wasteland.
> (20) The wild animals will honor me,
> jackals and dwellings of ostriches,
> because I give water in the desert,
> rivers in the wasteland,
> to give drink to my chosen people,
> (21) the very people I formed for myself,
> so that they might announce my praise.

After the reader is reminded again and again of the past greatness of God's creative and redemptive work, we are warned not to get stuck in the past! This God is the God of the new, the fresh, the surprising. Look carefully at what this new thing of God is to be: roads in the wilderness, rivers in the wasteland, water in the desert. Immediately we are reminded of Job 38:26, that announcement that the creator God is concerned about far more than humanity as God redeems the cosmos. The new thing of God is not limited to the history of Israel's redemption at the sea, nor will it be limited to the return to Israel from the Babylonian exile. The redemption of God is to be the redemption of all of nature, of which Israel is only a part.

This inclusive redemption is made certain by the mention of jackals and ostriches that will now "honor" the giver of water in the wastelands. These two creatures are regularly used, either singly or in a pair, (Mic 1:8 and Isa 34:13 as a pair and Isa 35:7; Mal 1:3; Jer 9:10, 10:22, 49:33, the jackal alone) as signs of desolation and wasted places. In God's new act of creation, these two animals of the wastelands will drink the life-giving water of God in the desert and will honor that God in the manner that we witnessed in Psalm 148 in the previous chapter.

And also as in Psalm 148, humans will join the animals in praise and honor of the creator who brings water to the chosen ones in the most unlikely of places, places previously haunted only by ostriches and jackals. We also remember that the ostrich was that silly and speedy creature, mentioned by God to Job, as an important part of the whole range of God's panoply of creatures, creatures that Job, and we, should value a great deal more as a reminder of our proper place in the cosmos of God.

This brief examination of creation and the prophets of Israel has reinforced the discoveries we have made heretofore in Genesis, the Psalms, and Job. We are God's chosen ones, but we are only a part of the larger plan of God for the redemption of all things God has made. We need to learn a greater sense of humility as we explore this larger plan in order not to exalt ourselves too highly in that plan, nor to treat as less valuable the vast range of creatures that are just as important in the plan of God as are we. Further, Second Isaiah has made plain that necessary connection between creation and redemption, between God's concern for the cosmos as the necessary context for God's concern for human redemption. After reading this poet, no longer may we assume that the salvation history of God has only human beings as its object; God's redemption and salvation are for all of God's creatures. And in the twenty-first century, this theological conviction has become far more than an intellectual one; it has become for us now, in our time of environmental peril, nothing less than a matter of life and death for us and for our fellow creatures.

SERMON

"Remember . . . but Don't Forget!" (Isa 43:14–21)

To remember is an important thing. I come home from work, and my wife asks me if I have remembered to stop at the store. I mumble, "I forgot," and there is no milk for the cereal in the morning. Remembering is important. We visit the memory loss unit at the assisted living home, and we see people who knew us well, but now know little at all. Remembering is important. Each time we take communion at the altar rail, we are bidden to "do this in remembrance of me." To remember is important.

Remembering is not just important for us Christians. Israel was asked to remember again and again. Four full columns of the Hebrew dictionary I use are given over to the meaning of the word "remember." The Bible asks us to remember what God has done in saving us, blessing us, commanding us. And on occasion certain psalmists ask God to remember what God has done for their ancestors in the past and urge God to do it again for them. Most amazingly, God's great servant Moses asks God, rather less than humbly, to remember God's own promises to Abraham, Isaac, and Israel. Moses asks this just as God is about to destroy the idol-makers of Sinai. Fortunately for them, God remembers and decides not to do it.

So when that unknown prophet of the Babylonian exile, whom we for convenience call Second Isaiah, reminds his fellow exiles about the past actions of God, we are hardly surprised. "Remember," he says, "how God created you and shaped you." Oh, yes, we say. We remember that God is our creator. After all, we say, "I believe in God the Father Almighty, maker of heaven and earth." "Remember," he says, "how I was with you when you passed through the waters of the sea, and thereby escaped the clutches of Pharaoh." We remember, they and we say. "Remember," he says, "how your enemies, all those mighty chariots and their horsemen, were drowned in the sea, while you walked safely through on dry ground." We remember, we and they say. We remember all those fine deeds that God did in the past, all the saving and redeeming and powerful actions and wonderful commands and on and on and on. We remember, we are grateful, we celebrate the God of the past.

But memory is not enough, is it? We cannot build a life on memory alone. We cannot live and thrive on memory alone. We treasure our memories; they help make sense of the present. But we live in the present. We need something more. We need something new, not just more of our memories, but something really new.

And Isaiah knows that, too. He knows that memories alone will not help us survive exile. He knows that memories alone will not be enough to carry us out of exile to a place we have heard of, hoped for, but never seen. Its newness and strangeness are terrifying. Better the familiarity of Babylon and its well-known high walls and massive towers, than the mysteries of the desert, that wasted place of howling jackals and peculiar ostriches. A place of long distances between watering holes. That dark, unknown, spooky, God-forsaken place.

So Isaiah announces a great surprise. Isaiah speaks the word we need to hear. God is not only a God of memory. God is a God of our present. God is the God of the new thing. And so Isaiah says, "Don't remember that old stuff, those familiar first things, because God is doing a brand new thing!" Have a look! That barren desert between us and home has just been crossed by an interstate highway! That blasted wasteland has just been drenched in the longest and wettest rain in living memory, and the desert has burst into bloom! And even the jackals and ostriches, the bad beasts of the wasted places, are now grazing quietly and baying and cackling their praises to God. God has acted in these new ways for all of us, for desert places, for jackals and ostriches, and for us. And the best we can do is join the chorus of praise to this God of the new.

Remember, he says, but do not get stuck in your memory. Do not think that the God you remember is the only way God can be. Far from it. Don't forget that God is ever-new, ever-fresh, so glaringly present that whatever deserts there are can bloom, whatever jackals there be can praise, whatever raging seas there are can be divided and safely crossed. Oh yes, remember what God has done. But never forget what God will still do.

5

"Woman Wisdom Has Built Her House"

Creation and Wisdom

Divinity is not playful. The universe was not made in jest but in solemn incomprehensible earnest. By a power that is unfathomably secret, and holy, and fleet. There is nothing to be done about it, but ignore it, or see.

—ANNIE DILLARD

THE WISDOM LITERATURE OF Israel has too often received short shrift in the study of the Hebrew Bible. It is only in the past twenty-five years or so that scholars have turned more focused attention on this most diverse of the sacred writings. The wisdom books usually are said to include Job, Proverbs, Ecclesiastes, and several Psalms (Pss 1; 34; 37; 49; 73; 127–28). In addition, two books from the apocryphal literature of the second and first centuries BCE, Ecclesiasticus (or Ben Sirach) and Wisdom, should be included. Also, many wisdom ideas and phrases have found their way into most books of the Hebrew Bible (see Isa 28:23–29 and Jer 17:5–11 as examples). Because I found Job to be so central to a full understanding of creation and our human place in it, I have already given over an entire chapter to it. Now I shall focus primarily on the extraordinary idea of Woman Wisdom as she is introduced to us in Proverbs. But first we should offer a definition of the term "wisdom."

Fretheim says,

> Wisdom is an inexact term that is commonly used to refer to knowledge regarding life that God has built into the infrastructure of the natural and social worlds, the search for those understandings in everyday experience, and the transmission of the results of that search.[1]

Given this definition, one can see that wisdom in the Hebrew Bible is far more than intellectual knowledge; there is a clear practicality to it. That is why Proverbs has as its most basic dichotomy the sharp distinctions between the wise and the foolish. The ability to live wisely is "built into the infrastructure of the natural and social worlds,"[2] into the whole creation of God. The refusal to search for this wisdom leads inevitably to foolishness, as anyone who lives in the world can easily see with her/his own eyes. One must seek this wisdom, which is more than just "head" knowledge, but one must also teach it to others. Truly to gain wisdom is to share wisdom; wisdom untaught is no wisdom at all.

Thus, the sages of Israel, moving well beyond the skeptical Athenian philosophers who confronted Paul on Mars Hill, according to Luke, urged their students to do much more than to spend "their time in nothing but telling or hearing something new" (Acts 17:21). The search for wisdom was often a search for the new work of God, but it was also the need to learn to keep awake to the world around in the attempt to discern that God-implanted wisdom in order to share that wisdom with all. And because this wisdom was the very glue that bound nature, God, and humanity into an interdependent whole, the search for it was crucial and ongoing.

Still, it was not enough for the sages of Israel to speak of wisdom in such an abstract and general way. Hence, the portrait of Woman Wisdom. The choice of making wisdom a female figure has crucial ramifications for the study of creation. This can best be seen in a closer look at Proverbs 8:22–31. In these verses we gain insight into the primordial creation of Woman Wisdom by YHWH, and we learn just how she stands at the very

1. Fretheim, *God and World*, 199.
2. Ibid., n57, 353.

heart of God's ongoing creation. The way that one chooses to translate the first two lines of this passage are very important for the understanding of this picture of Woman Wisdom.

> (22) YHWH begat me at the beginning of God's way,
>> God's most ancient work from long ago.
> (23) Long ago, I was poured out,
>> first, before the ancient earth.

A check of the NRSV will yield several significant differences in my reading. The verb in 22a is read by NRSV more generally as "created." However, the verb is used in Gen 4:1 to announce the birthing of Cain by Eve and at Gen 14:19, 22 to proclaim that YHWH birthed the skies and the earth. The image is certainly a feminine one. So also at 23a, the verb is read in NRSV as "set up," a possible reading, but the usual meaning of the verb is "pour out." In the light of the feminine birthing verb of verse 22, this verb could also be related to the breaking of the waters in the process of birth. God, as mother (see also Isa 42:14; 66:12–13 for other mother images for God), gives birth to Woman Wisdom at the "beginning" (the first word in the book of Genesis) of God's way; it was in fact God's most ancient work, before the creation of the earth. Verse 24 extends the idea:

> (24) When there was no Tehom, I was birthed,
>> before there were springs awash with water.

The word I have capitalized, Tehom, is that word usually translated "deep" as in Gen 1:2. It has long been known that this word is a Hebrew cognate with the Accadian goddess of creation, Tiamat. Before any waters were seen, before the goddess Tiamat was revealed, before the deep out of which God made the world's waters were in existence, Woman Wisdom was given birth by YHWH. In short, she was before the beginning of all things. Verses 25–26 continue that conviction.

But verse 27 changes the scene.

> (27) When God set up the sky, I was there;
>> when God drew a circle on the surface of Tehom.

Now Woman Wisdom proclaims that while God is in the detailed act of creating sky, delimiting Tehom, fixing the sky above and the springs of water below (vs. 28), setting boundaries for the sea, setting the foundations for the earth (vs. 29), she was there through it all.

But what exactly was she doing while God was this whirlwind of activity? Again the translation of the next verses is crucial.

> (30) I was beside God as a confidant;
>> I was a daily delight,
>> rejoicing before God always,
> (31) rejoicing in the whole creation,
>> and delighting in the human race.

The key description of Woman Wisdom is as a "confidant."[3] She has been birthed by the mother God to be an advisor, one who shares intimately in the creative work and then invites her followers to enter into the joys of that work. The NRSV's reading, "master worker" is attractive, but it has very little support from other biblical usage (see only a disputed text, Jer 52:15). The idea of Woman Wisdom as God's confidant allows her to play an important role as witness of and advisor to creation and then celebrator of that creation.

But her constant joy at the whole of creation, and God's thorough delight in her, are both crucial parts of her function as well. God found great pleasure in her as a partner in the ongoing work, and she, in turn, rejoiced in her mother God and rejoiced in the "whole creation." The NRSV's reading of verse 31a as "his inhabited world" I think misses the point of the unusual linking of the two nouns, *tevel* and *erets*. The former is often found as a poetic synonym of the latter, the common word "earth" or "land." But here they are side by side, augmenting and strengthening one another. Neither word implies human habitation. The meaning appears to be the "whole creation," that in which Woman Wisdom finds such joy. Added to that is her wonderful delight in the human race, those human inhabitants of the whole creation. Hence, her delight and joy are in all the cosmos, the creation of which she has just witnessed.[4]

---

3. William McKane, *Proverbs*, 356–58.

4. Is it possible that the author of these remarkable words had the divine plural of Gen 1:26 in mind? When God announces, "Let us make the human being in our image, after our likeness," this passage may suggest that God was conferring with Woman Wisdom.

Fretheim makes a valuable observation about this birthing imagery.[5] Certainly the unique ability of a woman to give birth made her both feared and held in high esteem by men. This extraordinary gift that allowed new life to be created again and again was the perfect metaphor for Woman Wisdom who represented, among other things, the "ongoing creational process," ever fecund and ever new. As she was birthed by God, so she could give birth to new possibilities for the ongoing creation that she both sees and delights in.

And Fretheim makes one other interesting observation concerning the femaleness of Woman Wisdom.[6] It is without doubt that the Israelite sages who offered this portrait of Woman Wisdom lived in a patriarchal world where men defined the political, social, economic, and religious norms of the community. Yet, the figure of Woman Wisdom, the confidant of God, who was with God from the beginning of all things, raises the work and way of the women in the community to the level of a norm. If the person of Woman Wisdom has been modeled on the roles of Israelite women in families and the larger community, namely as teacher and homemaker, then the famous picture of the Woman of Worth of Proverbs 31:10–31 is the very image of wisdom. By looking at her, we are looking at the essence of wisdom. Hence, Woman Wisdom in Proverbs offers us a new vision of how a society may be constituted. For example, Fretheim suggests that discussions of the correct use of power in community may be profoundly affected by the model of Woman Wisdom. "The power of wisdom is a power in, with, and under rather than power over; it is a power that is committed to the dynamics of genuine relationship."[7] Should not this view of power, arising from the person of Woman Wisdom, the very first work of God, not be employed to counteract those views of power, that "power over," that have so influenced human history?

And cannot that view of power help those of us who are searching for a new way to relate to the environment in which we live? Under the teaching of Woman Wisdom, we can learn to live with the natural world rather than strive to dominate it. Under her call to delight and joy, we can delight in the natural world rather than see it only as means for our ends. She still has much to teach us, if we but listen to her call:

5. Fretheim, *God and World*, 211–12.

6. Ibid., 210–11.

7. Ibid., 211.

(9:1)Woman Wisdom has built her house,

has hewn her seven pillars.

(2)She has slaughtered her food,

mixed her wine,

set her table.

(3) She has sent out her servant girls;

she calls from the highest places in the town,

(4) "You simpleton! Come here!"

To the senseless, she says,

(5) "Come, eat my bread,

drink my mixed wine.

(6) Put aside being a simpleton, and live!

Walk the insightful way!"

Still, we simpletons have a hard time following the way of wisdom. We do not know where to search for it, let alone know how to teach it to anyone else. For us there is a lovely passage in Isaiah 28 that might be of help. Dating this passage has always proven contentious, but it certainly comes from the pens of the sages. Whenever it was composed, and whenever it was inserted into the prophecies of the Isaianic school, it is important for those of us who want to search for the wisdom of God as it is found in the natural world and want then to teach that wisdom to others. Perhaps by implication it is Woman Wisdom who calls here.

(23) Listen and hear my voice;

pay attention and listen to my words!

(24) Do those who plow for planting plow all day?

Do they tear open and split their ground continually?

(25) When they have smoothed its surface,

do they not scatter dill, sow cumin,

plant wheat in rows,

barley in its place,

with spelt around the border?

(26) They are instructed correctly;

their God teaches them.

Here we are asked to learn proper living from the farmer who has been taught by God when to do certain actions when preparing and then planting a field. The farmer does not plow all day long, ripping and tearing at the soil. When the field has been smoothed off, the farmer plants the seeds in precisely the ways appropriate to each seed: dill seeds are scattered while cumin is sown; wheat seed is put into rows, barley seed finds its place, while spelt rings the field with its planting. A well-planted field is a teaching from the wisdom of God, and we simpletons can learn that our lives can also be well-planted if we attend to things appropriate to themselves, rather than forcing things to conform to ideas and practices inappropriate to them. But the teaching from the wisdom field is not yet over.

> (27) Certainly dill is not harvested with a threshing sledge,
>> nor does a cartwheel role over cumin!
>> Rather dill is beaten out with a stick,
>> and cumin with a rod.
> (28) Bread grain is pounded,
>> not threshed over much.
> One drives the cartwheel over it,
>> but does not smash it!
> (29) This all comes from YHWH of hosts,
>> who is wonderful in counsel,
>> and great with insight!

Again we can learn from the ways the farmer does and does not harvest the crops. The farmer does not treat the delicate dill and cumin with huge threshing sledges and heavy cartwheels. Even the hardy wheat grains for bread, though pounded, are not smashed into useless powder. Each plant is treated in the way appropriate for the harvesting of that plant. And this too comes from the God of wisdom, wonderful in counsel and filled with insight. And so the simpleton, searching for the wisdom of God, can find it in the planting and harvesting of a field. When Woman Wisdom calls, the simpleton may not always find the truth in books or from learned teachers in classrooms but on occasion from nature well-loved and well-tended. This passage beautifully illustrates the interdependence of wisdom and nature, of wisdom and creation. The pericope is a dialogue between and among the farmer and God, the farmer and nature, wisdom and the simpleton.

Woman Wisdom has built her house and is calling all simpletons to join her in the search for wisdom that is ultimately the search for the way of God. Is wisdom always so simple to be found? Hardly! Job 28 warns that only God finally knows the way to it. But that fact does not suggest that we should give up the search. Quite the contrary! The search for Woman Wisdom is the work of all of our lives. And though her power is, as Annie Dillard has it, "secret, holy, and fleet," to search for her, and on occasion to find her, is nothing less than life itself.

SERMON

"Why Should Woman Wisdom be Found?"
(Proverbs 8:22–36)

You and I are creatures of our language. We are as we speak. The various ways that I name you—friend, enemy, stupid, beautiful, fat, funny—go a long way to fixing you into categories in my mind. When God gave Adam the power of naming the animals that God was making, God gave Adam an extraordinarily powerful and dangerous gift. We should rethink that old school yard taunt: "sticks and stones may break my bones *and* names can really hurt me!"

We males have had it mostly our way in this business of language almost from the beginning of human speech, especially in languages that did not develop clear gender differences in their grammars. In English, for example, the word *man* came to stand for all human beings, and *his* grammatically included *her*. So it also was in ancient Hebrew where the basic word for God was *El*, a masculine noun, or *Elohim*, a masculine plural noun. Hence, all the pronouns referring to divinity in the Hebrew Bible are masculine ones. This naturally led readers of the texts to imagine God as a male, an image reinforced in iconographies of God through the ages, perhaps culminating with Michelangelo's muscled and bearded divinity at the center of the Sistine Chapel. This may be the single most recognizable picture of God in the western world.

Unfortunately, this exclusively male divinity has too often served as a wall against any other way of receiving the presence of God. If God is male, then males must be somehow better than females, more like God, stronger, smarter, more natural leaders, and on and on. And further, if God controls things, then males should naturally control things: women, other males, and the natural order. Now let's be frank: this male control has been less than a successful way to run a world! The history of humanity over the past few thousand years, marked by near universal male dominance, can hardly be judged a roaring success. We have just exited a century in which some two hundred million of our fellow humans were slaughtered in wars and uprisings, perhaps more than all the centuries preceding put together. And I fear that this estimate may be too low.

Let me be clear now. I do not for a moment think that if all power in the world were handed to women immediately at the end of this sermon, that everything would be instantly improved; we are all sinners, after all. Still, I have long wondered if a more balanced way to see the instruments of power, along with a more balanced way to witness to the power of God, might not be extremely helpful for all of us, for us humans and for our furry and leafy companions on the earth.

How about a seriously different model of God as seen in Proverbs 8? Traditional translations do not capture the feminine portrait painted in this chapter. Woman Wisdom, she who was brought forth by God before the making of the earth, is here describing her creation. Listen to the language she uses.

> YHWH birthed me as the first of God's way.

The verb used is the one used by Eve in Genesis 4 as she celebrates the birth of her son, Cain. Then Woman Wisdom adds,

> Long ago I was poured out.

Can this "pouring out" be a reference to the waters bursting from the womb as she is birthed by a God who is obviously here her mother?

What might we gain by celebrating God as mother? For many of us, the locution falls gratingly on the ear, because we have simply not heard it much. For others it sounds like a "political correctness" game where we all try to be inclusive so as not to offend anyone. But I want to say clearly that there is far more at stake than our hurt sensibilities or our faintly liberal attempts to include everyone.

We twenty-first-century Christians are in desperate need of conversion to a new way of seeing ourselves and the world in which we live. That means we are in desperate need of a new way of seeing the forces of power that drive the world in which we live. If God can be seen as a mother, giving birth to Woman Wisdom, she who witnesses and celebrates everything that God has created, might we then redefine what power is? If power is woman power, relational rather than controlling or dominant, working in and under the work of the world rather than always over it, our relationship to the creation of which we are a part can change. To view God more broadly can help us to view the natural world differently. To see God as mother as well as father can give theological weight to our needed conversion. This is only one way that a different view of God might help us all to speak differently and then to see differently.

How we talk about God is crucially important. It determines how we think about God. And how we think about God determines how we act in, with, and for the world. Let's continue to talk, but let us make our talk productive for our change. This God, who breaks all our limited boundaries of speech, bids us open our mouths in praise, not of the old and familiar but of the God who is ever fresh and new. As Paul says it, "The whole creation groans in labor pains in eager longing for the revealing of the children of God" (Rom 8:19, 22). Perhaps part of that new revealing will be a new way to speak of God. And as a result, the groaning world might find release from its pain, giving birth to a new world of hope for all of God's cosmos, loved and redeemed by Jesus Christ.

6

"In Him All Things Hold Together"

Creation and the New Testament Epistles

The 'key-log' which must be moved to release the evolutionary process for an ethic is simply this: quit thinking about decent land-use as solely an economic problem. Examine each question in terms of what is ethically and esthetically right, as well as what is economically expedient. A thing is right when it tends to preserve the integrity, stability, and beauty of the biotic community. It is wrong when it tends otherwise.

—ALDO LEOPOLD

THE DISCUSSION OF CREATION and its relationships to God and to us continues into the New Testament. It remains unfortunately still rare to encounter much commentary on these questions from scholars of the New Testament, though the references I quote in the next three chapters suggest that that is changing. Of course, the writers of the New Testament had always to reckon primarily with the multiple ways in which Jesus of Nazareth, who is also named Jesus Christ by the faithful, influences all theological discussions; he is the subject finally of all New Testament texts. Hence, it did not take much time for the apostle Paul, our earliest Jesus commentator, to begin to reflect on the vast implications that the coming of Jesus had, not only on his own life, but on the lives of all living things.

In his early letter to the Galatian Christians, he saw in Christ a new ordering of the world. The hierarchies of the Roman society were now null and void in the Christ.

> (3:27) As many of you as were baptized into Christ have clothed yourselves with Christ. (28) There is no longer Jew or Greek, there is no longer slave or free, there is no longer male and female; for all of you are one in Christ Jesus. (29) And if you belong to Christ, then you are Abraham's seed, heirs according to the promise. NRSV

Here is a radical claim indeed. Those baptized into Christ now belong to Christ. And all who belong to him are now seeds of Abraham, who received the promise of God long ago to be father of nations, child of God, founder of God's chosen people. And once you are in Christ, your identity as Jew, Greek, slave, free, male, or female no longer has ultimate meaning for you. Your ultimate identity is now in Christ. As Paul will later tell the Corinthian church, "If anyone is in Christ, there is a new creation; everything old has passed away; see, everything has become new" (2 Cor 5:17)!

Paul, in these initial reflections, sees clearly the impact of Christ's coming on him and on the emerging Christian community. Indeed, after the coming of Christ, humanity can never be the same. And when these reflections are placed into the political context of a completely Roman world, the implications are far more than spiritual ones. If Jews and Greeks, if slaves and free, if male and female, are no longer fixed in their hierarchical places, no longer determined by birth to live and act in certain predictable ways, then the political implications are volcanic.

These comments are common enough in the study of the radical Paul whose explosive impact on the world of humanity has been well documented. However, Paul's restless and searching mind did not stop with the impact of Christ's coming on human community. For Paul, Christ has affected all things in heaven and on earth.

To the Corinthians, as Paul rings the changes on his burgeoning understanding of the impact of the resurrection in 1 Corinthians 15, he of course reflects on the importance of Christ's resurrection for human believers (vss. 1–23). But then his language expands outward as he reflects further on the eternal work of Christ in the universe. It turns out that

Christ "must reign until he has put all his enemies under his feet" (vs. 28). The last enemy to be destroyed is death. Though Christ's resurrection has drawn the sting of death (vs. 55), the final end of death is Christ's ultimate work. Even death itself will be subjected to him. "When *all things* are subjected to him, then the Son himself will also be subjected to the one who put *all things* in subjection under him, so that God may be all in all" (vs. 28). This astonishing idea says that Christ's role is to bring *all things* (*ta panta*, in Greek) under his subjection; he is to be Lord of all. Yet, when that finally happens even he, Christ, will be subjected to the one who allowed that work to occur, the God of all creation. So finally God will be "all in all" (*panta en pasin*). It will not be the final time that the phrase "all things" will be used to summarize the work of God in Christ in the epistolary literature of the New Testament.

I would suggest that Paul in speaking to the Corinthians in this way has merely begun his expanding thinking about the work of Christ in the cosmos. That rich and deepening reflection continues in Paul's final letter to the Romans. In the remarkable chapter 8 of that letter, Paul raises the level of his metaphorical thought to poetic heights still unsurpassed in Christian writing. As he thinks of his ministry of some twenty years, encompassing dangerous journeys of ten thousand miles and more, on leaky ships and on robber-ridden roads, faced by continuous opposition from within and without the new communities he has founded, he stares eternity in the face and writes:

> (18) I think that the sufferings of this time are not worth comparing to the glory about to be unveiled to us. For the creation waits with eager longing for the unveiling of the children of God . . .
> (22) We know that the whole creation has been groaning in labor pain until now; (23) and not only the creation, but we ourselves, who have the first fruits of the Spirit, groan inwardly as we wait for adoption, the redemption of our bodies.

Though there is some dispute about the meaning of "creation" (*ktisis*) in this passage, it appears to be referring to the whole of non-human creation.[1] If so, Paul here ties the redemption of all of creation into the work of Christ's redemption. The whole creation waits and groans, in the same way that we humans wait and groan for the adoption of Christ through the power of God. Christ's work is now not merely a work for us; it is a

---

1. Cullmann, *Christ and Time*, 103.

work for the entire cosmos. It could be said that Paul implies here that the restoration of a fallen cosmos, just like the restoration of a fallen humanity, has been accomplished in the work of Christ.

The fact that this meaning of the passage is a likely one is made certain by the earliest commentary on the letters of Paul, namely the post-Pauline letters of Ephesians and Colossians.[2] In the Ephesian letter, the author extends Paul's notion in Romans 8 that the work of Christ is finally for the whole of creation.

> (8)"In all wisdom and insight (9) God has made known to us the mystery of God's will, according to God's pleasure set forth in Christ, (10) as a plan (or "community") for the fullness of time to gather up *all things* in Christ, things in heaven and things on the earth."

The implications of this passage for the restoration and redemption of the whole creation in Christ are well summarized by Elmer Flor.

> The term *ta panta*, moreover, embraces all components of the cosmos, physical and spiritual. This 'summing up of all things in Christ' ultimately implies this intrinsic worth extends to all creatures, and therefore the need for those who know the Cosmic Christ to reflect the same attitude towards creation, working with Christ to redeem 'all things'.[3]

In short, if we claim to be "in Christ," and claim to be new creations in him, we are by necessity lovers of the whole creation of which we are part, and are called to work for its restoration as Christ works for it. This is the New Testament's way of saying what Leopold said at the head of this chapter: that which leads to the integrity, beauty and stability of the creation is right and is quite literally of Christ whose work is the same.

Yet, the ultimate epistolary expression of this Pauline idea is found in the first chapter of the post-Pauline letter to the Colossians. Every lover

---

2. Though there remains considerable and voluminous debate concerning the authorship of these two letters, I hold with those who consider both of them post-Pauline. See Bornkamm, *Paul*, 86; Furnish, "The Letter of Paul to the Ephesians," 834–35, and Furnish, "The Letter of Paul to the Colossians," 857–58, albeit with less conviction about non-Pauline authorship. See also Roetzel, *Paul: The Man and the Myth*, who has no doubt that Paul did not write either of the letters and is joined in that conclusion by Cousar, *The Letters of Paul.*

3. Elmer Flor, "The Cosmic Christ and Ecojustice in the New Cosmos (Ephesians 1)," 143–44.

of the environment who is at the same time a Christian would do well to have Colossians 1:15–20 committed to memory.[4]

> (15)He is the icon (*eikon*, image) of the invisible God,
>> the firstborn of all creation,
> (16) because in him all things (*ta panta*),
>> in heaven and on earth,
>> things visible and invisible,
>> whether thrones or dominions,
>> whether rulers or powers;
>> all things (*ta panta*) have been created through him and for him.
> (17) He is before all things (*panton*),
>> and all things (*ta panta*) hold together in him.
> (18) And he is the head of the body, the church (*ecclesias*).
>> He is the beginning,
>> firstborn from the dead,
> (19) so that he might become himself preeminent in all things (*en pasin*),
>> because in him all (*pan*) the fullness of God was pleased to dwell,
> (20) and through him to reconcile all things (*ta panta*) to himself,
>> making peace by the blood of his cross,
>> whether things on earth or things in heaven.

This immensely rich passage calls out for more time than I can give it here. But several observations can be made. First, the "all things" idea of Romans 8 has become the leitmotif that binds the pericope together. For the author of Colossians the work of Christ is now seen as thoroughly all-encompassing. No fewer than seven times in these verses do we read variations of the word "all." He is before "all things," "all things" have been created through him and for him, he is preeminent in "all things," and by him "all things" hold together. In short, this punctuated litany of all things explodes the work and word of Christ into the origins and sustenance of the entire cosmos. Just as God in the Hebrew Bible, as we have seen, is both creator and ongoing sustainer of the universe, so here is Jesus Christ described in the same role.

Second, the theme of pre-existent Woman Wisdom, that we witnessed in Proverbs, now finds its exemplar in Jesus Christ. Of course, this theme is also to be found in other places in the New Testament (see John

---

4. My reading of the passage owes much to Bouma-Predinger, *For the Beauty*, 105–10.

1 and Hebrews, for examples). But here in Colossians the idea that Christ exists prior to creation, yet also is supreme over it, is put to the task of demonstrating his redemption of creation by reconciling all of it to himself by the blood of his cross. How far the author of Colossians has moved from the early Paul of Galatians 3:28 and his concern merely to describe how the event of Christ has altered forever all human hierarchies!

Third, the author makes, especially in verse 16, an audacious and dangerous claim. It is commonly stated that the references here to "thrones, dominions, rulers, and powers" mean heavenly principalities, divine forces that Christ overcomes in his great work.[5] Such an understanding is clearly not incorrect, given the way these words are used in other places in the New Testament. But given the context of this writing such a view can only be partially correct.

In a thoroughly Roman world, a world where Rome was preeminent in all things political and social, words like "thrones and rulers" must surely have had a quite practical political effect, as well as a more spiritual one. To announce in exalted poetry that Christ himself is the very image of the invisible God would have proclaimed to the cities of the east, those cities in and near Colossae (see Sardis, Pergamum, Thyatira), that their vast cult of the Roman emperor, whose images graced great temples for all to see, were in fact little more than a sham. Only Christ is the image of God! Further, any pretensions about rulers and thrones having anything to do with Roman leaders are equally foolish. Since all things have been created, sustained, and ruled by Christ alone, no other rulers need apply; the job of lordship has been filled for all time. In the same way that Jesus is remembered in the Gospels to have challenged the pretense of Roman power, albeit on occasion more subtly, so the author of this letter states categorically that the claims of Rome are null and void.

Fourth, the means that Christ chooses to reconcile the cosmos to himself, including us to him, are most peculiar, most especially in the context of a Roman understanding of power, the famous Pax Romana. The success of Roman power was based on the careful deployment of the

5. For example, Furnish, in the *Interpreter's One-Volume*, says that the letter is designed to correct the "errant teaching" that claimed that all must escape the "principalities and powers" that "exercised demonic control over all human life," 856. The hymn of verses 15–20 is only concerned with fate and angelic forces. Furnish mentions no political implications. Moule in *Peake's Commentary on the Bible*, 990–91, agrees, though he believes that Paul probably wrote the Colossian letter.

Roman legions and the ongoing myth that Rome was finally unbeatable in battle. "Peace" was then based on acceptance of Roman hegemony, a willingness to do as Rome asked, thereby avoiding inevitable Roman wrath. But this Christ ensures the reconciliation and restoration of all things through the "blood of his cross." What finally does that mean? Bouma-Prediger says it well:

> This peace is secured not through violence or conquest or the merciless bloodletting of others . . . This is a different peace—the shalom of the kingdom of God—and a very different peacemaking—one in which a person voluntarily suffers for others and in so doing absorbs evil.[6]

The intimidation of the Pax Romana is rendered moot by the gift of the life, death, and resurrection of this Christ, who reconciles the cosmos to himself and to itself by his act of self-giving.

Fifth, the redemption of the cosmos is its restoration, not its annihilation. This is a crucial insight in the twenty-first century where too many Christians are being led to believe that the ultimate work of Christ is a destroying work rather than a work of reconstitution of the cosmos.[7] The author of the Colossian letter wants his readers to know that Christ's great work is the restoration of the world to that place that came fresh from the hand of God. Because Christ is "firstborn of all creation" and "firstborn from the dead," his work is to glue back together the broken fragments of the world of Genesis 1 and thereby to reconstitute the *shalom*, the unity and oneness, that God had in mind at the creation.

The implication of that construal of the work of Christ is that salvation is not some sort of escape into another and better world, a Gnostic breakout from the evil prison of earth. In Christ, we look for the reclamation of the earth, and in Christ we dedicate our lives to that work, as Christ himself leads us in that work. Christians affirm nature and cosmos, they do not pray that at the coming of Christ all will be destroyed while they are saved. The author of Colossians would be the first to raise an alarm against those who do not hold the cosmos in the deepest reverence and who do not pray and work for its reclamation and return to *shalom*.

6. Bouma-Predinger, *For the Beauty*, 108.

7. See again the two works of Timothy Weber noted earlier for a readable history of the belief held by many modern Christians that the end of the world and time will include the destruction of the cosmos.

As we can see, both Paul and those who learned deeply from his work, have continued the creation theme of the writers of the Hebrew Bible. Their understanding of Christ led them ever deeper into rich reflections on the theme of creation and the many ways that Christ's work intersected with the creation and sustenance of the cosmos. To be sure, any Christian worth the name will follow her/his Lord and love the cosmos and work for its renewal and its future as a necessary Christian task.

I am an ordained United Methodist and am rightly proud of the ways in which my denomination has tried to be responsive to the issues that confront us all and to do so by taking very seriously the work of theology. Our Book of Discipline, setting out our social principles, as well as the myriad rules that govern the work of our church, rightly contains a section on The Natural World, section 160 of the Social Principles.[8] Here are its opening words:

> All Creation is the Lord's, and we are responsible for the ways in which we use it and abuse it. Water, air, soil, minerals, energy sources, plants, animal life, and space are to be valued and conserved because they are God's creation and not solely because they are useful to human beings.

Unfortunately, perhaps tellingly, this 2000 version of the paragraph omitted a very important and powerful sentence that appeared in the 1980 Discipline. "Therefore, we repent of our devastation of the physical and nonhuman world." This call to repentance should resound in our churches each Sunday. We too often repent generally from some general notion of sin for which we too often receive a too-general forgiveness. Such a transaction is so vague as to be meaningless. Little wonder that real repentance comes rarely to our lips. But without this specific repentance of "our devastation of the physical and nonhuman world," there can be for us no conversion to the work of Christ with the cosmos. Surely all the evidence before our eyes calls out for such repentance. The whole cosmos is groaning, awaiting the unveiling of the children of God. It is high time that those children showed up.

8. *The Book of Discipline of the United Methodist Church 2000*, paragraph 160.

SERMON

"The Real Work of Christ" (Colossians 1:15–20)

How did we ever get to this sort of Jesus? This friendly friend? This beach buddy? This sweet little guy who cares only about my soul, my place in eternity, my personal relationship with him, my intimate knowledge of him, my tight little, quiet little, personal little connection to him? Just when was it that that Jesus first showed up? Could it be that he first appeared when I decided that all that really mattered were my decisions for myself, and that when push came to shove I decided what was right for me and what I did on my own was nobody's business but my own? When what I thought, and what I bought, and what I did, and what I said were only a matter of my own individual choice? Was that when old solitary, personal, individual Jesus first came around?

Well, I really do not quite know when he came. But I do know this. He resembles the Jesus of the Bible hardly at all! This quiet little buddy who "walks with me and talks with me, and tells me I am his own," is a sweet romantic fellow, but I hardly recognize him in the mirror of the Scripture. That Scripture Jesus is often loud and often outspoken, yea, downright offensive at times. And he seems hardly at all interested in individuals only; in fact he is forever getting into trouble because he keeps making groups decidedly uncomfortable. I mean after all, would anybody get nailed to a Roman cross for being real sweet to individual people? I don't think so. In fact I know so.

Well, what's the problem here? Can't we preachers just leave us with this nice-guy Jesus, who urges us to be kind and gentle and pleasant to humans and beasts, a sort-of Dr. Phil of Palestine, smiling as needed but on occasion tough enough to tell each one of us, one at a time, what we ought to do? Well, can't we?

If you have guessed that the answer to this question for me is No, you are quite right. I will tell you what the problem with this sort of Jesus is for you and for me. Like most nice friends, you can take him or leave him, depending on your particular needs or decisions. He really is rather dispensable, don't you think? I mean if I am making all the decisions anyway, why can I not just decide to toss old buddy Jesus aside when he does not fit my need today? I need a bigger Jesus, a vaster Jesus, a Jesus more deeply engaged in things far larger than I. Because if he isn't any larger in his concern than just me, well, maybe he is rather too small in the long run to be very effectual at all.

The author of the letter of Colossians needed a very large Jesus indeed, and, thank God, he found him. Colossae was a place right in the heart of the Roman empire in the east. And it was in that part of the empire that the Roman emperors had their greatest success in convincing their subjects that they were somehow divine beings. Their images dotted the cities of Asia Minor, announcing in indestructible marble that Rome ruled the world and always would rule the world.

But this author noticed something that I learned on my last trip to Corinth, many hundreds of miles west of Colossae, but still a seat of Roman power. In my several trips to this part of the world, it was a commonplace to see that so many of the statues of the Roman nobles were headless (this is particularly true at Corinth). Our guide made this clear to me just this year. The statues, she said, were made with removable heads, rather like marble Mr. Potato Heads, I thought! They did so to save money. Power changed hands so rapidly, that it was far cheaper to have a new head made for the newest power broker than a whole body. As Shakespeare has it, "Uneasy lies the head that wears the crown," and the Romans made interchangeable headless statues accordingly.

Let's get clear about all this nonsense, says the Colossian writer. There is only one preeminent one, only one lord of heaven and earth, only one firstborn of the dead, only one who is creator, sustainer, and redeemer of the cosmos. He is Jesus of Nazareth, Jesus the Christ, Jesus the Lord of all things. Jesus is not your little soul buddy, your individual guru, your personal confidant in the dark watches of the night. He is the master of all things, the creator of the cosmos. He is far more than I can get my own little head around. And that is very important to me, personally.

Like the author of the letter, I live in a world where the ways of this Jesus are much talked about and little done. I live in a world of a new Pax Romana, a sort of Pax Americana, or maybe better a Pax Stuffiana. Buy and eat and consume as much and as rapidly as possible, because you don't live forever and you might miss a piece of cake, or a TV extravaganza, or a beautiful place in the world, or the right watch, the right car, the right friends, the right church, if you don't hurry up to get it. Consume is the name of our game. And the lowly environment may take the hindmost. I mean, the oil and the soil and the air and the water and the sun and the moon and the stars are merely backdrops for my desires. I decide how they are to be used; I decide where they are to go. I drive and eat and go and use whatever I want whenever I want. And Jesus is my friend; he loves me, and I love him. Well?

If Jesus is larger than the Pax Romana, making that attempt to intimidate the world foolishness, and if Jesus is larger than my personal desires for certain clothes or food or cars, then maybe he makes all of that foolishness, too. Maybe the Pax Stuffiana is just as dumb as the Pax Romana. And if Jesus is creator and sustainer, the Lord of all things, then maybe he is not merely my buddy. Maybe what he wants to be is my Lord, yet not just *my* Lord, but the Lord of all at the same time. The writer of this letter says seven times in six verses that Jesus is over all things. All things. No, Jesus is not just my buddy; he is my Lord, and because that is true, the way I live my life, all of it, all of it, is under his direction. So go ahead. Ask what Jesus would drive, what he would eat, what he would buy. Because if you don't, he will just be your buddy, and you can discard him, ignore him, relegate him to your attic anytime you would like. But if the writer of Colossians is right, then he is Lord of all things. And if that is so, now what?

7

"Look at the Birds of the Air"

Creation and the Gospels

It is in midwinter that I sometimes glean from my pines something more important than woodlot politics, and the news of the wind and weather. This is especially likely to happen on some gloomy evening when the snow has buried all irrelevant detail, and the hush of elemental sadness lies heavy on every living thing. Nevertheless, my pines, each with his burden of snow, are standing ramrod-straight, rank upon rank, and in the dusk beyond I sense the presence of hundreds more. At such times I feel a curious transfusion of courage.

—ALDO LEOPOLD

JOHN'S JESUS MEMORABLY SAYS, "I come to bring life and bring it abundantly." And by such abundant life he apparently means both a life of eternity with God and with him as well as the quality and richness of an abundant life right now. It could be said that this promise and hope are the very essence of the content of the Gospels of the New Testament. They have been read, perhaps from their very origins, as statements of Jesus' work on behalf of the human race. Whatever references there may be to nature and the natural world in these Gospels are at best mere backdrop to the drama of human salvation wrought by the life, death, and resurrection of Jesus of Nazareth. In short, they have been read in much the same way that the Hebrew Bible has been read, as a story of human sin and salvation, the "historical" activity of "God with *us*."

But we have seen in the previous chapters that the theme of creation is far more prominent in the Bible than has usually been recognized, most especially in our readings of the Hebrew Bible. Yet, even the epistolary literature offers crucial and powerful witnesses to the theme, witnesses from which we may still learn significant theological lessons for our new century. As we saw in chapter 6, it was the apostle Paul, and his letter-writing heirs, who made the imaginative theological moves that expanded the Jesus movement into a much larger vision of a cosmos-restoring reality.

But now in this chapter we must ask: is there much talk of the natural world, the cosmos, in the gospels of Jesus? I think the answer must be: yes and no. There is little doubt that the gospels are centrally concerned with the work of Jesus for you and me. We human beings and our reconciliation to God are the focus of the work of Jesus, as the Gospels present his story. Yet, a careful look at some specific passages will reveal that there are significant things to be said about the natural world in relationship to the life of Jesus. We will examine Matthew 6, Luke 12, and John 1-3. I do not suggest by these choices that these are the only places where such natural world concerns may be found in the four Gospels, but they appear to be the places where we may discover valuable work for our topic.

It is very easy to romanticize Jesus' loving concern for those lilies and the companion "birds of the air."[1] In such a reading, Jesus is turned into a first-century St. Francis, enamored with the natural world, using it for beautiful and sweet sermon illustrations from which we all can learn lessons for our lives. Then it is pointed out that Jesus often uses homey agricultural images as examples, most especially in his parables. Thus, it has been concluded that he is aware of and in love with the natural world: sermon point—so should we be! Take time to smell the roses and listen more attentively to the song of our feathered friends.

---

1. Santmire in *Travail*, 200, warns of this danger. "Jesus and his proclamation are to be viewed accordingly in terms of the world of apocalyptic thought for our purposes here. His apocalypticism, then, not his celebrated—and often romanticized—concern for the lilies of the field and the birds of the air, is the critical point to be underlined as we pursue the theology of nature given in his life and his teaching."

Though there may be a small grain of truth in these saccharine reflections, a closer look at the way Jesus actually is said to employ the birds and the lilies in this passage yields a far more robust understanding of nature, of its intrinsic value to God, and its importance to us.

A 2002 article by Adrian Leske offers a helpful analysis of Mt 6:25–34.[2] Leske first makes the obvious point that the pericope is primarily about anxiety, a state that can only be eased if we seek "first the realm/rule of God and God's righteousness" (Mt 6:33).

> Clearly, the point being made is that God feeds the birds of the air *even though they neither sow nor reap nor gather into barns* (Mt 6:26), and the grass of the field is beautifully adorned *even though the flowers neither toil nor spin* (Mt 6:28). Thus the central point being made is that one enters into and accepts God's kingdom and his righteousness as God's gracious gift, and then all these things will follow from this relationship.[3]

"God's righteousness" is not here "the sum total of what God requires as a prerequisite for entering the kingdom,"[4] but is instead the certainty that God supplies whatever is needed to live in the world ruled by God. This is, in fact, *God's* righteousness, not ours. As the Gospels always want to say, we respond righteously only after we have received God's righteous gifts for us.

Now that we understand that the passage is speaking of God's gracious gifts, we can further see, in the light of a passage from Deuteronomy 28:47–48, that this part of the Sermon on the Mount is intended to reverse the curses hurled at the unfaithful Israelites in the final Deuteronomic sermon of Moses.[5]

> (47) Because you did not serve YHWH, your God, joyfully and with a good heart for the abundance of everything, (48) you shall instead serve your enemies, whom YHWH will send out against you, in hunger and thirst, in nakedness and lack of everything.

---

2. Adrian M. Leske, "Matthew 6:25–34: Human Anxiety and the Natural World," 15–27.

3. Ibid., 19.

4. Betz, *Sermon on the Mount*, 483–84.

5. Leske, "Matt 6:25–34," 21.

The book of Deuteronomy is a series of sermons with one basic point: God has given Israel everything it needs to flourish in the land of promise primarily because God loves Israel uniquely (Deut 7:7–8). Still, in the body of the sermons there are numerous places where warnings are given to those who refuse the blessings of God. Such refusal will lead to curses: loss of land, hunger, thirst, nakedness, etc.

But in Jesus' sermon in Matthew 6 there is a reversal of the curses of Deuteronomy, and even more, a promised renewal of the world. Leske says, "Matthew 6:33 is really a declaration of the fulfillment of the prophetic longings for a future restoration and a complete reversal of Deuteronomy 28:48. No longer is there to be hunger, thirst or nakedness. The phrase, 'all these things shall be added to you' (Matt 6:33), incorporates all the blessings of relationship and harmony in God's realm."[6]

And that insight brings us to our concern with the natural world, because the passage "expresses the blessings of harmonious relationship with all of nature, expressed in Deuteronomy 28:2–6. The time of restoration has come. The kingdom of God is here. They now live under the covenant blessings, no longer under the curse."[7] The great promise of God's renewal of the entirety of the natural world, including the humans who are part of it, that we have seen in the Hebrew Bible and in the letters of Corinthians, Romans, Ephesians, and Colossians, is reiterated here. The choice of birds and grass is important, because they are both of so little monetary and physical value in our eyes. Birds are two-a-penny in the marketplace (Matt 10:29), while grass has only the briefest span of existence. Yet, because "God knows the fall of every sparrow" (Matt 10:29) and dresses the grass so beautifully, "there can be no room for anxiety about clothing in the kingdom of God."[8] As we saw earlier in the Psalms 19 and 148, nature speaks, albeit silently at times, of the wondrous goodness of God and the intrinsic value of bird and grass, so magnificently arrayed and cared for by the gifting creator.

Of course, the primary concern of Matthew 6:25–34 is the divine-human relationship, but it is no less significant to read in these lines the implied kinship with all other members of the world of creation. A closer look at them, and a deeper appreciation of their place in the cosmos, can

6. Ibid., 23–24.

7. Ibid., 24.

8. Ibid., 25.

teach us of the gifts of the creator, the one who cares for all of creation and has called all of it very good.

The parallel passage in the Gospel of Luke reinforces these positive notions for a robust ecotheology, but it also offers a warning that needs to be taken seriously by environmental readers of the Bible. Luke introduces his version of the "consider the lilies" passage with the dramatic story of the greedy farmer. The farmer's land is so productive that he is faced with a dilemma; his storage spaces are too small to hold the huge abundance he has received. His solution is to tear down the inadequate barns and to build bigger ones, large enough to store both his grain and his goods (Luke 12:18). Surely there is irony in his use of the generic word "goods" (*agatha*). In what sense are these unnamed things "good"? Why should he store them in his new huge barns? Grain is clear enough, but just what are these goods? Whatever they are in particular, they enable the farmer to look forward to a future of luxurious living. "And I will say to my soul (*psyche*), 'Soul, you have many goods stored up for many years: rest, eat, drink, rejoice!'" (Luke 12:19). The ancient equivalent of a substantial 401K with assured interest moves the farmer toward a comfortable retirement, perhaps some golf, punctuated with some exotic travel.

But the voice of God intervenes with the harsh claim that those greedy ones who act like this are "fools" whose souls are demanded "this very night " (v. 20). The implication of the phrase is that all of our souls are finally demanded *every* night. And then the shocking intrusion is capped by the haunting question, "And those things you have hoarded—whose will they be?" Once one is dead the goods go to strangers, other greedy folk, the IRS, the probate judge, whomever. And Luke adds in verse 21, "So it is for those who store up stuff for themselves but are not rich to God." The last phrase could mean that greedy folk who think they are rich, and by the world's standards are rich, in God's eyes are not rich at all. And it also means, of course, that "being rich to God" is something completely different than having bigger barns stocked with grain and goods.

And what that means Luke makes clear by his version of the lilies and the ravens. I have spoken above of the positive value that this passage has for our view of the environment, but I now want to note a problem that could move us in the opposite direction. Three times in the passage (and once in the Matthean version) human beings are represented as being of more worth than the non-human creation (12:7, 24, 28). As has long been noted, the rhetoric here represents an example of the rabbinic "*qal wachomer*" or "how much more so" style of writing. But that rhetorical observation in no way alters the fact that ravens, lilies, and field grass are explicitly said to be of less *worth* than humans. I consider this to be an important and dangerous problem for our attempts at conversion toward a new way of understanding our human relationship to our non-human earth partners. Both Matthew and Luke make our environmental job harder by these formulations, and the fact that the sayings have become an intrinsic part of the language, indeed a clichéd part of the western world, compounds the problem for us.

We should not, of course, deny the very useful environmental implications of these passages. The rich farmers' greedy excess is a continual warning against our greedy exploitation of the earth's resources to feed our insatiable desires for riotous pleasure. The marvelous fact that God is ever attentive to and deeply caring of the non-human creation (birds, lilies, grass) is a reality to be celebrated. And the fact that we are called into a similar attentiveness and caring is a hopeful sign that we can look to as we move toward our conversion toward the *shalom* of the cosmos. But if we continue to follow the passage in its direct valuation of the non-human creation as less than we humans, we may be sidetracked in our movement toward envisioning God's cosmos in the new ways to which I have suggested we are called. We should always remember that not everything the Bible says may be ultimately helpful as we consider God's creation. And this ambiguity of possible usefulness of the Bible for a view of the environment is continued in the Gospel of John.

The literature on this extraordinary book is enormous.[9] It has been examined in so many different ways as to beggar description, but since our purposes have to do with the Gospel's possible concerns for the natural order, its intrinsic value, and our human relationship to it, we will examine it in two very different, and in many senses contradictory ways. In short, there are those who find enormous support for a positive

9. The marvelous twelve hundred page commentary of Brown, *The Gospel According to John,* remains indispensable, but massive works on this Gospel make regular appearances. Three examples are: Carson, *The Gospel According to John,* 715 pages; Morris, *The Gospel According to John,* 824 pages; Ridderbos, *The Gospel According to John,* 721 pages. The fact that the same press could publish two 700+ page commentaries on the Gospel within two years (!) indicates the huge importance this Gospel possesses in the academy and the church.

ecological reading of the Bible in the Gospel of John, and there are those who find this Gospel a challenge for such a reading. To examine these two approaches, I will focus primarily on chapter 1.

It is a commonplace to say that John 1 has been heavily influenced by Genesis 1. In the latter God creates at the beginning sky and earth and calls forth from earth the plants and animals and the humans to form a balanced, ordered, and structured design, based on the interrelated unity of *shalom*. All of this creation is called very good (Gen 1:31). In the Gospel, the Word of God exists at the beginning, and that Word, that *logos*, was with God at the beginning, creating "all things" (v. 3). And in the fullness of time the Word became "flesh and pitched a tent among us," "full of grace and truth" (v. 14). It is perhaps from John 1:14, in addition to John 3:16, that proponents of a positive view of the natural world find their support. The Word becomes Jesus, an actual human being, living as one of us; though clearly divine, the Word became human. And the reason for that incarnation is offered at John 3:16: "God loved the cosmos so much that God sent the only-begotten son, so that all who believe in him may not perish but have eternal life." If God is so in love with the "cosmos," and if the cosmos means the entire created order, then surely the gift of God's son, the living Word, is designed to do what the first chapter of Colossians announced. As in that letter, the role of Jesus is to restore the cosmos to its originally intended wholeness. Surely this is a possible and positive reading of these famous passages.

However, there are those who find these words troubling for an ecological reading. For example, Norman Habel, editor of the five-volume series, *The Earth Bible*, finds in the gospel of John a possible earth-rejecting dualism. He argues concerning Genesis 1 that "nothing in the physical universe, either in its primordial or ordered state, is negative, alien or evil. All of the Earth community pleases God who declares it good."[10] But in the Johannine worldview there are basic dualisms that are absent from the Genesis world. For example, the light and dark of Genesis are both necessary parts of the design of the cosmos, while in John the light is good and the dark is evil. C. M. Carmichael, in a study of John 1, claims that "Jesus is the light that appeared at the creation," a fact that he then contrasts with the constant negative claims for the darkness made by

10. Habel, "An Ecojustice Challenge: Is Earth Valued in John 1?," 78.

John, most famously at 1:5.[11] Habel concludes, "Carmichael's study seems to confirm that John is not interested in the physical world of creation, but the spiritual reality that comes into creation with Word as revealed in Jesus."[12] Habel sees in John a very basic dualism between physical and spiritual, a dualism where the physical is denigrated and left behind by the spiritual work of the one who comes from above and returns there, drawing all believers to himself.

For Habel, then, the incarnation is not designed to redeem the natural world that is in fact only a temporary "abode of Word passing through from 'above' to 'below' and back to 'above' again."[13] Even if the transcendent Word enters the material world, it does not stay there; it does not redeem the material world. Thus, the material world cannot be accorded the same value as the spiritual world that is the final goal of the Word and all who would follow the Word. For Habel, the Gospel of John could prove to be a hindrance to those who are pursuing a world-affirming, earth-friendly theological ecology. And I think it fair to say that much of the use of the Gospel of John has moved toward a spiritual view of the divine Jesus, the God-human who speaks at a different level than his speaking partners in his dialogues, who knows all that is to happen well before it does happen, who acts as the God he is clearly portrayed to be. And this portrayal often stands in the way of seeing the human Jesus. Fairly or not, this has often been the portrait depicted of Jesus in John's Gospel.

Still, Habel has not answered the challenge of John 3:16–17 where Jesus' work is said to be for the "cosmos." Even if the dualisms of John are real, is not the gift of Jesus given out of God's love for the cosmos, the whole of creation? Vicky Balabanski offers an analysis of "cosmos" in the Gospel.[14] After noting that the word occurs seventy-eight times (versus a total of only fifteen times in all three Synoptic gospels), she claims the word in John has a "shifting semantic value," and suggests four different meanings:[15]

11. Carmichael, *The Story of Creation: Its Origin and Interpretation in Philo and the Fourth Gospel*, 46–47.

12. Habel, "An Ecojustice Challenge," 80.

13. Habel, Ibid., 82. Santmire makes a similar claim in *Travail*, 212–13.

14. Balabanski, "John 1—the Earth Bible Challenge: An Extra-textual Approach to reading John 1," 89–94.

15. Ibid., 90.

1. It is the context into which humanity comes and lives (Jn 1:9, 10a) (She reads these verses as the NRSV footnote reads them; "He was the true light that enlightens everyone coming into the world (*kosmon*)": see the Fourth Edition of the United Bible Societies Greek New Testament.)

2. It means the totality of creation (Jn 1:10b as parallel to Jn 1:3)

3. It means the world of human affairs (Jn 10c)

4. It means "this world" as contrasted with a world above (Jn 8:23; 18:36)

Then she asks which one of these meanings, or which combination of them, should be applied to John 3:16–17. Most Johannine commentators (she claims that *none* she has read!) consider the possibility of God's action in Christ having any other interest than a human one, and that is to be expected when humans are those in the Gospel who are under judgment for sin but who are capable of belief. However, through the lens of ecological concern, and given the multiple possibilities of the meaning of the word "cosmos," there is no objective reason to reject her meaning 2 as a part of the meaning of the word in these verses.

The implications are as follows: First, God loved the totality of creation so much as to offer the son as the locus of possible human belief and human eternal life. However, that human belief is not confined to meaning 3, the world of human affairs only, but must be extended to the totality of creation, all of which is loved by God. Jesus was not sent merely because of God's love for humanity alone. Second, God did not send the son into the human world only, but into the totality of creation, and not for the purpose of condemnation or rejection or denial of the totality of creation, but in order that the totality of creation might be made whole through the son. That would imply that our human belief in the son must by definition lead to our work toward the restored wholeness of the creation, since it was that creation, that cosmos, and God's love for it, that engendered the coming of the son in the first place. When read like this, the classical understanding of the incarnation, "God with us," must be extended to "God with the Totality of Creation."[16]

And then we might rewrite the opening sentences of the Nicene Creed (as well as many other popular creeds) in something like the following way:

16. Ibid., 91–93.

We believe in one God,

the Father and Mother (see chapters four and five above),
the Almighty,

maker of heaven and earth,

of all that is, seen and unseen.

We believe in one Lord, Jesus Christ,

the only son of God,

eternally begotten of the Father,

God from God, Light from Light,

begotten, not made,

of one Being with the Father and Mother;

through him all things were made.

For the salvation of the totality of creation, including us,

he came down from heaven,

was incarnate of the Holy Spirit and the Virgin Mary

and became truly human.

Until we can enshrine these biblical ideas into our publicly stated claims of faith, our conversion to lovers of and workers for the natural order cannot be made real. In our public worship, and in our private lives of prayer, these ideas must find a place.

SERMON

"Consider the Lilies" (Matt 6:25–33)

There are any number of Bible phrases that have wormed their way into our everyday speech: the good Samaritan, the rich young ruler, the patience of Job. You can surely name some more. "Consider the lilies" is one of those. Don't worry, says Jesus, about what you will eat or drink or wear. Just consider the lilies, how they grow, and how they do not work at all, yet how handsomely they are clothed, so handsomely as to make Solomon himself look like a buyer off the second's rack at Target. Yes, just take a gander at those lilies.

Now, why exactly am I to look at the lilies? I mean, I like lilies. They are sure pretty at Easter time, their trumpet flowers blaring out the glad tidings of resurrection. I just love them in a grand profusion, pushing and shoving their white heads in the breezes of spring. But I am not to look at them because they are beautiful, says Jesus. I am to gaze at them because they don't do any work, but look like a million bucks anyway. Is that the point? The lilies are just like some trust-fund kids my son knows in Los Angeles; they don't do any work, but their fabulously wealthy parents load up the bank account so they can always buy Gucci and wear, well, whatever is the hot style today. So, I look at the lilies so I can dream that I might be like them, gorgeous but lazy? I don't think that is it either.

But maybe I am getting closer. Consider the lilies, says Jesus, because as beautiful as they are—and they are!—they sure do not last long. My wife and I planted a potted Easter lily some years back, and the thing bloomed in our yard the next year. My, were we pleased and surprised! But that was it; come the next year after that our blooming lily was all bloomed out and returned to the soil whence it came. In point of fact, no flower lasts for very long, and no individual flower is worth all that much really. I mean, you can always grow some more. And in Jesus' day, you could buy birds in the market two for a penny. And the grass of the field. Well, it hardly lasts at all and is only good for fuel—today in the field, tomorrow in the oven. Birds and grass, less than a dime a dozen.

Consider the lilies, says Jesus. They don't last long, and they aren't worth much by our standards of worth, but my, they are lovely anyway. And those birds! They are all over the place, and they come cheap, but they do sing well. Do you know that Texas mockingbirds can sing up to 30 different songs? But birds don't sow or spin or gather into barns grain for the winter, like you do. And lilies are just lilies; no sowing or spinning for them either. And the one-day grass, filling the fields with waving beauty one day and burning in the oven the next. No human work for them. So have a peek at the lilies and the birds and the grass.

Why? Because God gives them to us free. And God makes them beautiful for free. They are a vital part of God's vast and wondrous creation, even though they don't sow or spin or gather anything up. No, Jesus does not want us to look at the lilies and find there our calming gurus. You don't paraphrase this phrase with "slow down and look at the lilies." We have some things to learn from the lilies and the birds and the grass, and here they are. They are all pure gifts from a God who loves them and us all. And they are beautiful and interesting for no particular reason except that God is into beauty and interest. And another gift of God is presented in verse 33. "Look first for the kingdom and its righteousness and all of that other stuff, the food and the drink and the clothes, will come right along, too." God's righteous gift is God's love of lilies and birds and grass and you.

And if you and I can live in harmony with the lilies and the birds and the grass we really won't have to worry anymore about food and clothing and drink, and neither will our friends who are poor and forgotten and oppressed. The key is that we have to find God's righteousness right here among us now. And when we find it, we need to practice it for the whole of creation. Consider the lilies, says Jesus. And until I can see them for what they are—signs of the free gift of the rule of God—they will be, well, only lilies, instead of what they really are: God's lilies, God's gifts, God's signs of God's rule over and love for all creation.

8

"I Saw a New Heaven and a New Earth"

Creation and the Book of Revelation

Instead, therefore, of globalizing the market and profit mechanisms, we need to globalize other cultural values, such as solidarity, collective compassion for victims, respect for cultures, sharing of goods, effective integration with nature, and feelings of humanity and mercy for the humiliated and offended.

—LEONARDO BOFF

NO BIBLICAL BOOK HAS been more ill-used that the Revelation of St. John. After the rise and increasing popularity of so-called dispensationalism,[1] the book of Revelation became the lynchpin of elaborate beliefs in the Bible's encoded predictions of the fate of the world. In the past 150 years numerous authors have mined the scriptures for clues concerning the shape of the present and the architecture of the future. From John Nelson Darby to Herbert W. Armstrong to Hal Lindsey to Tim LaHaye, and a host of lesser-known textual detectives, millions of modern Christians

1. Latest statistics say that Hal Lindsey's *The Late Great Planet Earth* has over twenty-five million copies in print in thirty-two languages. It was until recently the best-selling single title, except for the Bible, in the history of publishing. It has now been outstripped by the wildly successful Left Behind series by Jerry Jenkins and Tim LaHaye.

have become convinced that the keys to the smallest details of all of our futures are to be found in the pages of the Bible.[2] Despite more than two hundred years of biblical research that has attempted to place each biblical book into its unique historical setting, in order that it may be first fairly examined as a product of its own time, these latter-day, would-be prophets have reaped a huge harvest of ardent believers, not to mention buckets full of cash.[2]

Such readings of the book of Revelation, based on little more than a fevered imagination, coupled with a thin veneer of pseudo-scholarship, have in effect removed the book from the inspection of numerous thoughtful Christian people. The mere mention of Revelation brings responses like: "scary" or "spooky" or "esoteric nonsense." The fact that it is off-limits to many is bad enough. But the more dangerous result of these predictive readings is two-fold. First, the first-century intent of the book's author to confront the power of a demonic empire with the power of the Christ is completely avoided. If the book only predicts a future of apocalyptic destruction, then its call to examine the horrors of economic and social empire, and its dire environmental implications, in the first century, and then in the twenty-first century, goes unheeded. Second, the modern political implications of the predictive readings, with the state of Israel at their center, creates a potentially monstrous understanding of the role of military and economic power as they are applied to the Middle East. In short, if Israel must exist as one of the necessary signs of the predicted second coming of Christ, then defense of the state of Israel must be undertaken at all costs, notwithstanding the complex role that the state of Israel plays with the Palestinians in their midst, as well as its role with the Arab states in its geographical context. This preferential option for Israel, at the expense of its neighbors, is at least in part the result of these beliefs in Israel's role in the apocalyptic drama ascribed to the book of Revelation.[3]

2. Just this past weekend, May 21, 2011, an aged engineer convinced any number of gullible followers that the second coming of Jesus was "certain" on that date, based on his careful calculations from the Bible. The fact that I am still writing indicates that once again Bible calculations have proven to be flawed. This of course will hardly be the last attempt at such mumbo-jumbo.

3. Weber, *On the Road*, chap 6, "The Founding and Expansion of Israel," 155–86. See also the more nuanced reading of the relationships between Israel and the dispensationalists in Spector, *Evangelicals and Israel*, 2009.

I reject these predictive readings of Revelation completely. They are based on nothing but air and break the most basic truth that any reading of an ancient text must take with the utmost seriousness: the text was written by some particular someone (or someones) at some particular time for some particular audience. No reader can avoid that reality and thereby create the text in her/his own modern image. The author of the Revelation did not write his book to us; we moderns can only overhear what he wrote to others. The fact is that we can read the book of Revelation in its own context and can understand, with a fair measure of certainty, just what John had in mind when he wrote his extraordinary tract against the Romans and on behalf of Jesus Christ. And what John had in mind is especially significant for our concerns with the environment.

The book of Revelation is actually "about" two related things: the dangerous struggles of John's present, namely, the fight against Roman hegemony in all things, and the assured good future of God's victory over Rome and all empires who aspire to be Rome.[4] We will focus our attention on chapters 21–22 to illustrate these two ideas.

> (21:1) And I saw a new heaven and a new earth, because the first heaven and the first earth had disappeared, and the sea no longer existed. (2) And I saw the holy city, the new Jerusalem, that is always descending out of heaven from God, made up as a bride adorned for her husband. (3) And I heard a loud voice from the throne saying, "Look! The tent of God is among human beings. God will tent with them, and they will be God's people. Even the living God will be with them, will be their God! (4) And God will wipe away every tear from their eyes. And death will no longer exist: mourning and crying and pain will cease to be, because the first things have disappeared."

Several features of this passage are important for our cosmic concerns.

1. This culminating image of John's revelation begins with a "*new* heaven and a *new* earth." The double use of the word "new" has led many readers to envision a brand new creation here, one completely discontinuous with the old earth and heaven. Then these readers have determined

---

4. There are fortunately numerous valuable studies of Revelation that work from these suppositions concerning its first-century context. One of the very best remains Caird, *The Revelation of St. John the Divine;* see more recently, the comprehensive commentaries of Aune, *Revelation, Three volumes* and Blount, *Revelation.* Valuable articles may also be found in Schüssler-Fiorenza, *The Book of Revelation: Justice and Judgment.*

that this new heaven and earth is some sort of unearthly and spiritual place, lined with golden streets, floating untethered, a land "up there" and far away. But this is not the only, or the most natural, way to understand the vision. What John means by "new" is "renewed." In keeping with the grand vision of Isaiah 65:17–25, surely John's inspiration for his vision, God does not mean to obliterate God's creation in a hailstorm of flaming meteors and apocalyptic wind (nuclear blasts?), and then start all over. Eugene Boring says it well; "God does not make 'all new things,' but 'all things new.'[5] John sees the future of God as a decidedly earthy one;[6] God fulfills creation's promise and does not destroy it. The feverish nightmares of divine destruction of the earth that will be witnessed by the raptured ones in the clouds, as portrayed by the dispensationalists, are precisely the opposite of God's future desire for a redeemed and renewed earth. To view the vision like this is to demonstrate that our responsibility for the environment is itself God's own call to us to join God in that work, a work that will be fulfilled in the wondrous future of God.

2. In the vision the heavenly and the earthly places are forever joined together as one; and God will live with us and with all of God's creation for all time. God's place has always been with creation, and likewise in the new heaven and earth God's home will be there forever. For those of us who strive to commit ourselves to the work of God now, the image of the descending holy city is especially instructive. At first reading, we might imagine that the city's descent from God is an act only for the distant future. However, the choice of tense for the verbal participle, "coming down," is unusual. It could be heard as an "iterative present, denoting a permanent attribute of the New Jerusalem."[7] That is, the Holy City is "always" coming down (hence my translation above), is always available to be seen by those who have committed themselves to the work of Christ, living by faith in his life, death, and resurrection. Walter Russell Bowie's 1909 hymn, "O Holy City, Seen of John," captures this aspect of the vision with special insight. Here is his verse 5: "Already in the mind of God that city riseth fair: lo, how its splendor challenges the souls that greatly dare; yea, bids us seize the whole of life and build its glory there."[8] This holy city

5. Boring, *Revelation*, 220.
6. Bouma-Prediger, *For the Beauty*, 114.
7. Caird, *The Revelation*, 279.
8. 726, *The United Methodist Hymnal*.

is not merely a future dream; it is a present reality for those with eyes to see; it is a continuous gift of God for the old earth and the new.

3. In the new heaven and the new earth evil and all its terrible results are banished. The sea, the place from which come the beasts of chapters 12 and 13, which served as the throne for the whore of Babylon (17:1), disappears, thus cutting off the doorway through which these vast evils entered the world. Mourning, crying, and pain are no more, and death itself no longer exists. In the new heaven and earth there can be no place for the whore of Babylon, who is in fact Rome, as 17:18 makes plain. And then in chapter 18, Babylon/Rome falls and with its fall the exploitative economic power of the old world ends. At its fall the only ones who weep and mourn are the "kings of the earth" whose luxuries disappear (18:9), the wealthy merchants whose supplies dry up (18:15), and the sailors who transport all these goods (18:17–18), among which were the abominable human cargo of slaves (18:13). All music ceases, all art, all food production (18:22). The lamps are doused, weddings stop, because the truth is that the whole economic system was built on deception and the blood of "prophets and saints" who had called the system into question by their faithfulness to God (18:23–24). And now it can be readily seen that the new heaven and the new earth are a repudiation of the current earth and its economic system, a system unconcerned with justice, inattentive to the God of creation whose desire for the cosmos is *shalom*. The mourning and wailing stop, because the exploitative economic engine is stilled. The sound heard instead in the new heaven and earth is the great multitude singing, "Hallelujah! Salvation, and glory, and power to our God, whose judgments are truthful and righteous. God has judged the great whore who corrupted the earth with her fornication" (19:1–2).

4. Moving on into the rest of chapter 21, the new heaven and the new earth contain a most unusual city (21:9–21). It is incomprehensibly huge, fifteen hundred miles square, surrounded by a wall forty-four cubits high (perhaps two hundred seventy feet). The city is gold and its wall jasper and encrusted with precious jewels. But its sheer size and unimaginable wealth are not what make it odd. Unlike all ancient cities of any size, it has no temple because its temple is "the Lord God the Almighty and the Lamb" (21:22). God and Christ no longer need a building in which to dwell because they are now tenting within the great city in every place. Neither is there sun or moon, as the new earth returns to its origin in Gen

1:1–13, prior to the sun and moon's creation (21:23). No need any longer for the lights of the sky, because God is now the light of the city forever and the Lamb is the eternal lamp. Night never comes to this city, and the kings of the earth are bringing their glory into the city via the gates that are never shut (21:24–25)! The last time we saw the kings of the earth they were wailing at the destruction of the whore of Babylon and the loss of their luxuries (18:9), but now in the new heaven and earth and its completely open city, they bring their glory into it. It is important to realize that these are the same kings who earlier were corrupted by the wiles of the whore of Babylon, an agent of the Beast. Caird comments,

> "Those who once brought the splendour of their luxury trade to deck the great whore now bring their willing tribute to adorn the holy city. Nothing from the old order which has value in the sight of God is debarred from entry into the new. John's heaven is no world-denying Nirvana, into which men may escape from the incurable ills of sublunary existence, but the seal of affirmation on the goodness of God's creation.[9]

John's understanding of God's goal for the cosmos matches that of the Matthean Jesus and Paul and his letter-writing heirs. God wills *shalom* for the cosmos, is always working toward that goal and bids us to follow. And 22:1–5 puts the seal on this certain goal.

> (22:1) Then he showed me the river of the water of life, bright as crystal, flowing from the throne of God and the lamb (2) through the middle of its street. On either side of the river is the tree of life, bearing twelve kinds of fruit, producing its fruit each month. And the leaves of the tree were for the healing of the nations. (3) Nothing accursed exists there, but the throne of God and the lamb will be in it, and God's slaves will worship God. (4) They will see God's face, and God's name will be on their foreheads. (5) And there will be no more night; they need no lamplight or sunlight, for the Lord God will be their light, and they will be in God's realm forever and ever.

At the last, agricultural images abound, and memories of Genesis and Ezekiel fill the background of the drama. Ezekiel 47:1–12 imagines a life-giving river that flows out of a restored Jerusalem temple to renew the acrid waters of the Dead Sea, causing it to swarm with fish. And along the

---

9. Caird, *The Revelation*, 279.

banks of the restored sea there are trees bearing fruit each month of the year, and the leaves of the trees are saturated with healing properties. John borrows the image, but extends its meaning, employing ancient imagery. Now the river is the river of the water of life and the tree the tree of life (see Gen 2:9–10). With the reader's mind planted firmly in Genesis, the fruit reference is reminiscent of the first couple's consumption of the fruit prohibited by God. But here in the new heaven and earth, the fruit grows "every month," no longer heeding the seasonal production of fruit, while the leaves that covered the naked fruit-eaters of Genesis, leaves that were signs of disobedience and shame, have become leaves for universal healing. Rivers and trees and fruit, the rich gifts of nature, are here sources of unrestricted food and refreshment and healing. The earth has been restored to its "very good" state, God's curse in the garden has been removed, "for the whole creation has been renewed by the re-creating hand of God; and no flaming sword bars the way to the tree of life."[10]

The restored earth, now joined with heaven, is further portrayed by two other images. In verse 3 "slaves now worship God" in the new place. The last we saw of these slaves they were crammed in the holds of the ships of Babylon/Rome, being transported to enrich the kings, merchants, and sailors of the empire (chapter 18). Now they are free to worship in the new realm of God and the lamb. Further, the blasphemous name of the Beast that was tattooed on the right hands and foreheads of any who would participate in the evil economy of empire (the number of which was the living number of the archetypal emperor, Nero[11]) has become the name of the living God stamped on the foreheads of the inhabitants of the Holy City.

To reduce these glorious images to some sort of crystal ball, parsing ever finer possible times and dates and nations to populate a projected drama of apocalyptic destruction for the billions and salvation for the few, seems little less than blasphemous itself. While shifting guesswork attempts to identify the Beast (the pope? Hitler? The European Common Market? The United Nations?), God causes the descent of the Holy City

10. Caird, *The Revelation*, 280.

11. The identification of the land beast with the emperor Nero is well-argued by Caird, *The Revelation*, 174–75. Though this reading is persuasive to many, it is hardly the only possible one. Given the ancient number game, *gamatria,* (wherein letters equal numbers) apparently being played here, it is of course possible that many solutions to the puzzle might be given.

as a daily reminder of what God has in store for the creation. At the last, there will be a vast city whose gates are never shut, and in which you will find a surprising collection of God's creatures, from kings to slaves, along with a river and a tree and continuous fruit for healing and wholeness for *all the nations*. Those who pray mightily and fervently for annihilation for the evil ones, and salvation for themselves, will be astonished, says John, to find themselves in the same city as those whom they judged evil.

The Bible ends as it begins with a vision of *shalom*, a vision larger, more wondrous, more inclusive than any can conjure. It is a vision where water and trees and fruit are an integral part. The Bible will not allow us to dream of a final escape into a denatured heaven, a mystical place peopled only by disembodied souls. We pray with the authors of Genesis 1–2, Psalm 148, Job, Amos, Hosea, and Isaiah, Ephesians, Colossians, Romans, Matthew, John, and Revelation that God will renew the earth and restore it, and us, and our fellow earth partners, to the wholeness and hope of our interdependent divine creation.

SERMON

"Living in the New Heaven and the New Earth" (Rev 21:1–5)

If the John of Revelation could talk, I imagine that he would say something like this: "Enough already! I want no more foolishness about what my words mean to you in the twenty-first century. Stop your chatter about Russia (where?), about Israel (what?) about who the Beast is for you (it is Nero, you dummy! Don't you get it?). Why don't you try to understand my world, instead of getting stuck in your own? Do you think that my words meant nothing to anyone until you came along? I mean, how arrogant can you get? To quote old Eliphaz in the book of Job, "Are you the firstborn of the human race?" So, pay attention, and I want to try again to help you get what I was getting at. Now, I know nearly two thousand years is a long time, and some of my writing may be a tad obscure, but if you get your head out of your own stuff for a while, you can get it. I promise. So, listen up! Here goes.

"I wrote this book late in the first century when the Romans ran everything. They controlled what we ate, where we lived, what we wore, where we traveled, and most of all, they tried to control whom we worshipped. Their power was unmatched, and they thought it was unrivalled. In that they were wrong. We Christians, growing secretly sometimes, quite publicly at other times, had other ideas about power. We were convinced that Jesus of Nazareth, who was the slain Lamb, dying on a cross in order to show us whom to worship, and how to live and possibly die, had the real power in the world.

"So when the Romans came to our towns in Asia Minor (that's Turkey to you twenty-first-century types), they told us, sometimes under pain of death, to worship the emperor, many of whom thought they were some sort of god. Ridiculous, of course. I mean there were so many emperors, and they changed so fast, how could they all be gods? A reign of three months or so did not inspire anyone to believe in one's divinity! But the Romans brought their statues (headless, so they could change heads with the change of emperors!) and demanded that we worship. They really thought that we were so stupid as to do it! But if we didn't, they made our lives hard. Without the emperor's tattoo we could not buy or sell, and they had their eyes on us all the time.

"I wrote what I did from a Roman prison on this little treeless island called Patmos. Isolated and quiet it was, but my heart was filled with the power of Jesus Christ, whom I had preached all over Asia Minor, and filled with the need to describe the Romans as they really were. I had lots of images to choose from, because I knew my Bible (that's the Old Testament to you) backwards and forwards. Genesis was especially good, Daniel had his helpful words, and the prophet Ezekiel had the sort of vivid imagination that I had. So I filled my book with many of their images: clouds and angels, and bowls and trumpets, and beasts and rivers and trees and fruit and on and on, there was no shortage of ways to say what I wanted to say.

"And what was that, you ask? I will tell you. The Romans were not what they thought they were. They thought they were running the world; they thought they would never be defeated; they thought their empire would go on forever. They were wrong on all counts. God and the slain Lamb run the world, I said. Not only will Rome not run the world forever; their doom as empire is assured. And the reason for that is quite simple; everything they do is opposed to the will and way of God. Their power comes from an evil source, what I call the Beast. I described this Beast as clearly as I could, but you knuckleheads could not get who I had in mind. He had seven heads and ten horns and seven diadems on his heads, all numbers of perfection, and you took me too literally! My description in this style was of great beauty, not ugliness. Why do you suppose the whole world followed the Beast with wonder? Because he was so attractive, so seductive, so desirable. And I gave him the number 666, calling it a 'human number' so that you could know it was a human being we all knew. I grant that this parlor game that we all played you no longer play, but here is what I had in mind. If you give the awful emperor, Nero, his full name, it is Neron Kaisar. If you transliterate that into Hebrew script, you get—ta da—666, since Hebrew letters are also Hebrew numbers.

"Now I know that Nero died at least 30 years before I wrote, but his memory was so powerful, and so terrible, that I thought he would make the perfect example of a real Beast. Unfortunately, being a Beast did not die with Nero; many Beasts came after him. I imagine you have known a Beast or two in your own day; perhaps even you have your beast-like qualities. But all that is secondary to the full truth; the beast loses, the empire does not last. The slain Lamb defeats the terrible Beast. That is basically what I had in mind.

"But, so what, you say? Well, if you lived in a time where one group lorded it over another, controlled every facet of life, determined who lived and died, bought and sold whoever and whatever they wanted, you too would need some certainty that such horror would not go on forever. That is what my writing is about, too. Where is all this going? Does God have anything to do with all this? Answer: God has everything to do with it.

"And so, since I understand that some of you, and I hope an increasing number of you, have special interests in the environment in your time, let me draw some implications for you. God is concerned about far more than just you and your human family. I know this because God is creator of all and renewer of all. I am convinced that God's basic business is restoring the whole cosmos, broken especially by God's human creatures, to its 'very good' state of the beginning of it all. And if that is so, then all of God's creatures must have a place in this restored cosmos, what I call, along with my colleague Isaiah, the new heaven and the new earth. Now don't get confused about this, as some of you less capable ones obviously have. God is not, repeat not, going to annihilate the earth, saving a few who say the right words or believe the right doctrines, and blast the rest with hot fires and howling winds. Such nasty nuttiness I can hardly conceive! Think of a city, a really big city, big enough for all people, I mean slaves and kings, and think of the gates of the city never shut (I know it is hard given the scariness of your day and mine!). Then think of a river of life and a tree of life, and fruit year round, and leaves for the healing of all nations. That is the goal of God. You and I and a whole bunch of people completely unlike us, and water and trees and fruit and leaves and animals, the whole created thing together at last, interdependent at last, one at last under the rule and love of God. And that goal, that vision, is constantly available, if you only have eyes to see. If you can get your eyes off empire and its wealth and ease and comforts, built on oppression and cruelty and death. It does not have to be that way, and it will not be that way forever. You can count on that!

"Look up! Go on, look up. The Holy City of God is descending from God just as it does every day. It is God's city, and all are welcome. But if you don't want all to be with you, then you may not be welcome. There are no exclusions here, no special treatment here. The gates are open to all. So come on and add your voice to the praises of God whose will for the whole cosmos is the wonder and certainty of *shalom*."

9

Preaching Creation

For just as the rain and snow fall from the sky,
    and do not return there without watering the earth,
    causing it to bear and sprout,
    giving seed to the sower and food to the eater,
So shall my word be that goes out from my mouth—
    it will not return to me empty;
    it will surely do what pleases me,
    and succeed in the thing for which I sent it.

—ISA 55:10–11

THIS PASSAGE IS ONE of the Bible's "preacher verses." Preachers need to keep these words in mind whenever they walk, run or stagger to the pulpit. When they open their mouths once again to do the unthinkable—speak for God—it is words like these that will make that task bearable or on other occasions downright horrifying. If I can be sure that God's word will be effective, will not return to God empty, regardless of the incompetence and/or unpreparedness of the day's preacher, I can be relieved of the burden that I will never be able, on my own, to proclaim the word of God. On the other hand, the passage may lull me into the certainty that my efforts toward preparing a word from God will never be, on my own, adequate, so I can always rely on God's promise to take my poorly arranged nonsense and magically transform it into a word from God. The passage says more than both of these possibilities suggest.

It takes the rain to water the earth in order to make possible the appearance of seed and bread, just as it takes God's speaking to create the hope of the cosmos. In the same way, it takes the work of the preacher— prayerful attendance on the word, careful exegesis, wide and deep reading in the subject chosen, a rich awareness of the congregation that will hear, ongoing concern for the preacher's health and wholeness—in concert with the full assurance that God is in the experience, helping to bring it to fruition, to make a transforming preaching act possible. Such thoughtful awareness of my role and God's role in my preaching makes any genuine preaching possible at all.

In this final chapter I want to suggest several things that a preacher who is concerned to preach a word on the environment must consider before engaging in that important task. Of course, some of the suggestions will apply to any act of preaching, but special considerations arise when the subject of the environment stands central in a sermon. I will discuss the five steps a preacher needs to take and in the order in which I think they should be taken.

Prayerful Attendance on the Word. The need for prayer is much talked about, but, I fear, less acted upon. I will confess that I have often tossed off the Christian line, "I will pray for you," and have almost immediately forgotten to do so. Prayer seems the right thing to mention—after all, we preachers are expected to believe in prayer. If we claim to believe in a God who loves us unreservedly, and wants only the best for us, to speak to that God on a regular basis appears to be the least we can do to keep up our end of the relationship. However, questions like: "for what do we pray?" and "what do we expect to happen when we do pray?" are very complex and often contentious. Because my concern in this book is to energize you and me to love, cherish, and to preach about our love for the environment, I want to remind us again of Psalm 148, a discussion of which made up the bulk of chapter 2. I suggested there that all creation silently and vocally is in continuous twenty-four hour praise of God, and that we humans are asked to join our voices to this cacophonous chorus. Our praise to God, in the larger context of creation's praise of God, can serve as the bedrock of our prayer to God. Our prayer in this environmental mode should not first be a request to God for some thing or the other, although our prayers will want to ask God for some particular things later. But first we must join our fellow creatures, animate and inanimate, in the act of praise to the creator and sustainer of it all.

Since I have been a United Methodist clergyman for over 40 years, I have sung the great 1739 Charles Wesley text, "O For a Thousand Tongues to Sing," many more than a thousand times. It has stood first in Methodist books of hymns since at least 1780.[1] For a preacher concerned with prayer and the environment, no better text could be chosen to announce the cosmic power of, and the call for praise to, the Triune God. "O for a thousand tongues to sing my great Redeemer's praise, the glories of my God and King, the triumphs of his grace!" God, Christ, and Holy Spirit redeem and sustain the universe through the glorious triumphs of grace. And the seventh verse[2] (Wesley originally wrote 18 verses for this hymn), says, "In Christ, your head, you then shall know, shall feel your sins forgiven; anticipate your heaven below, and own that love is heaven." Wesley makes it clear in his poem that praise of God as Redeemer through Christ enables us to see "heaven below"—no need to wait to see heaven only after we die—since love itself is heaven. I hope you can hear the echoes of Colossians 1:15–20 in this verse, as heaven appears now among us in the love and grace of Christ.

But at this point we must be careful to move beyond the traditional way to hear a praise song like this one. Wesley's hymn, I am certain, was intended to reflect only the divine-human interchange of love, repentance and forgiveness. It is during a praise/prayer like this one, and many more like it, that the preacher who has been made aware of God's love for all things God has made must add this central concern to the conversation. We preachers can no longer limit our preaching to human sin, human forgiveness, human redemption. Our prayer and praise must be broadened to include the whole cosmos of God, and that for two reasons. Because, God has that concern, and because the cosmos is under serious threat due primarily to human sin. When we pray, we must forever move beyond the exclusive anthropomorphism of our interests. Such human arrogance and blindness can no longer be tolerated in the church of Christ.

1. See the note on the placement of the hymn in previous Methodist collections on the page preceding the hymn, No 57, in *The United Methodist Hymnal*.

2. No 57.

So after we have hymned the universal power of God in Christ, we can pray for renewed strength in the struggle to love and restore the world in which we live. We can pray that we can better learn to see and experience the vast reaches of God's creation and that we can learn to love it for itself, not simply for what it can do for us. For example, we need to pray that the horrendous destruction of the world's rain forests (25 percent lost in just the past twenty years) cease, not because with its loss we might lose medicines that could cure human disease, and not even because these vast canopies of glorious trees have been carbon monoxide "sink-holes," the veritable lungs of the atmosphere, taking in great quantities of carbon monoxide and breathing out life-giving oxygen as well as water into the air. As important as these possible losses are to us humans, our prayer needs to be directed to the intrinsic value of rain forests in and of themselves, their beauty and mystery, their deep darkness and dappled light, their astonishing array of animals and plants, all of whom who by virtue of their being and actions according to their kind praise their creator. Oh yes, we preachers need to pray, but our prayer must expand, beyond our own lives, the lives of our congregations, and the lives of the human race only. If not, we will not love the cosmos for which Christ came, and our people will not hear the good news of God, the creator and sustainer of all things.

Careful Exegesis It has been a given, ever since preachers first felt moved to exposit publicly the sacred text, that reading that text carefully is the foundation of any effective sermon. Of course, the theological affiliations of any particular preacher will in large part determine just how that exegesis is to be conducted. I assume that all would agree, whether fundamentalist or not, whether liberationist or not, whether postmodernist or not, that the actual words of the text need to be taken with the greatest seriousness. And since those words were not written with any modern reader in mind, those words must be explained, at least first, in the historical context of their own composition. That historical reading may not exhaust the possible meanings of those words for us (and for me they surely do not), but that reading should be done in every appropriate exegetical work.

But the work of exegesis is far more complex than the triumphant cry, "The Bible says . . . !" Each reader will necessarily read the words through his/her particular eyes; the several locations of the reader will largely determine just how the words are read.[3] Such a claim is thoroughly self-evident. Over the past forty years, various persons, who have traditionally been shut out of the academic reading of the Bible, have begun to read it and to announce what they have found. African-Americans, Asians, Latino/Latina, poor persons, women, and others from other social locations have read the same texts, formerly controlled by generally rich white men, and have heard the texts in ways those white men simply could not. The number of these readings is enormous, and is increasing exponentially. No serious exegetes can any longer assume that their reading is the only possible reading, however well they read the ancient languages, however brilliant their insights, however vast their knowledge of the ancient world. All of us now exegete at a table filled with voices completely unlike our own, voices we necessarily must hear if we are to approach the riches the ancient words contain. No preacher can any longer approach the pulpit without some serious wrestling with these different voices.[4]

This concern is especially true when we consider the Bible and the environment. In the next section I will suggest several books that an environmental preacher must know before taking this subject on. It must be said that this special concern is not very old in the literature; serious academic discussion spans barely twenty years. Still, a public issue like concern for the cosmos should draw the preacher toward the best of the work that has appeared. Fortunately, several excellent scholars from many fields have turned their attention to the subject, and the preacher should turn to them next.

Wide and Deep Reading in the Subject. As I briefly mentioned in the introduction, when I did graduate work in the Hebrew Bible in the early 1970s, the Bible's important concern for the environment, a concern I have briefly outlined in the preceding chapters, was practically nonexistent. In fact, the environment was often said to be contiguous with a concern for nature religion, a "pagan" idea that the Bible went out of its way to reject. The Bible was said to use the natural world only as a backdrop for the Bible's chief concern of God's love for and redemption of

3. I have addressed this question of exegetical location in "The Bible Becomes Literature: An Encounter with Ruth," *Word & World*, 130–35.

4. The literature on the subject is vast. A good place to start is The Bible and Culture Collective, *The Postmodern Bible.*

humanity. This book is hardly an attempt to deny that the story of human fall and redemption is not a significant theme of the Bible's pages, but I have attempted to demonstrate that that story cannot be seen apart from the larger story of God's deep concern for the whole of the cosmos. In the Bible, our redemption is inexorably bound up with the redemption of the entire cosmos.

A preacher will then need to "get up to speed" on this Bible theme. Older commentaries, those written before 1980, will be of almost no help in this regard, and unfortunately, even very new works show little interest. I suggest the following books as beginning points; the list is not exhaustive but representative only.

1. An older yet luminous volume is that of Joseph Sittler, *Essays on Nature and Grace*. In wonderful prose, Sittler lays out the concern for a theology of nature, and since he is a teacher of preachers as well as a theologian, he can serve as an excellent conversation partner for those who want to preach on this question.

2. H. Paul Santmire, a long-time Lutheran pastor, and long-time advocate of environmental concerns, has published widely on the subject of nature and theology. I would point to three of his books. *Brother Earth: Nature, God, and Ecology in a Time of Crisis* appeared in the year of the first Earth Day celebration of 1970. In this book Santmire begins a critical assessment of the ways in which the history of Christianity has either valued or undervalued nature, and to examine how those Christian approaches to nature have affected the ways in which nature has been viewed in human history in general. Santmire's fuller account, expanding and updating his earlier book, can be found in *The Travail of Nature: The Ambiguous Ecological Promise of Christian Theology*. This book remains the richest appraisal of the history of Christianity and its "ambiguous promise" toward nature. Much more detailed work on each of Santmire's necessarily brief summaries of three millennia of Israelite/Jewish and Christian views of nature needs to be done, but his work is invaluable as a roadmap for those wishing to make the historical journey. The book is dedicated to Joseph Sittler, "Pioneering Theologian of Nature." Santmire's third and most recent book is: *Nature Reborn: the Ecological and Cosmic Promise of Christian Theology*. Here again Santmire plows the same ground, but

feels he needs to do so because so few theologians seem to have taken up the ecological mantle. Much of this book will sound familiar to those who have read the 1985 volume, but it is written with an increased passion, driven by the increasing signs of ecological problems that need an immediate address. Each one of these important books, and especially all three together, can get a preacher's heart racing in the direction of love for nature and a passion for preaching about nature.

3. Another theologian who has demonstrated deep concern for the environment is John B. Cobb, Jr. In a 1972 small book, *Is It Too Late? A Theology of Ecology,* Cobb wrote what was described as "the first single-authored, book-length environmental ethics." (The book was reprinted in 1995 by Environmental Ethics Books of Denton, TX.) In the book Cobb urges a "new form of Christianity" to address the issue that he is convinced is the central one for humanity, and after twenty-five years between reprintings of his book, he remained convinced that adequately to approach the depredations of human assaults on the environment implies that "the major forms of past Christianity are inadequate to our needs and must be superseded."[5] Cobb is an advocate for a kind of process theology that helps him, more than a more traditional theology, to address the problems of nature. Though you may not find his theological reflections always to your particular liking, this brief book is still very valuable to read as you prepare to preach on the environment.

4. Leonardo Boff, a Brazilian liberation theologian has written *Ecology and Liberation* wherein he joins the twin concerns of a theology of the oppressed to a theology of the environment. In fact, Boff offers the paradigm of ecology as an "infinite web of all-inclusive relations. . . . Ecology reaffirms the interdependence of beings, interprets all hierarchies as a matter of function, and repudiates the so-called right of the strongest."[6] Any theologian of liberation, anyone concerned especially with the wretched of the earth, must at the same time be concerned with the assaults against nature; the two are necessarily of a piece. To read this short book is to be made aware that a concern for the earth does not at all preclude a concern for the poor of the earth or vice versa.

5. Cobb, *Is it too Late?*, 4.
6. Boff, Ecology and Liberation, 7.

5. An excellent summation of much of the work represented by the books mentioned above may be found in the engaging volume, *For the Beauty of the Earth: A Christian Vision for Creation Care* by Steven Bouma-Prediger. In very imaginative and creative prose, the author goes over much of the ground found in Santmire, Sittler, and Cobb, but does so in several intriguing and memorable ways from a wonderful poetic reuse and update of the book of Revelation (pp 111–13) to the effective use of recent statistics concerning population growth, rain forest loss, acid rain, carbon emissions, among other up-to-the-minute environmental concerns. The second half of his hyphenated name means "preacher" in German, and no preacher can fail to be helped by this excellent book.

6. A fascinating series of five volumes from *The Earth Bible Project* (2000-2002) has appeared, all edited by the Hebrew Bible scholar, Norman C. Habel. Habel is based now at Flinders University in Adalaide, Australia as a Professorial Fellow in the Centre for Theology, Science and Culture. Each volume contains up to fifteen essays, all attempting to address specific texts of the Bible from the perspective of earth. Each writer (they are a wondrous array of scholars and native peoples from the four corners of the globe) was asked to do their reading in the light of six ecojustice principles developed by the Earth Bible Team. Briefly the principles are: intrinsic worth of all things in the universe; all things are interconnected; earth has a voice that can be raised against injustice; all things in the universe have a purpose for the whole; we humans must see ourselves as mutual custodians, rather than rulers; we and earth must be resisters against injustice. The seventy-four essays in the five volumes cover many specific texts from both testaments. I readily admit that it was this series of books that rekindled my passion for this subject, and I urge you to dip your toe, if not your whole body, into the rich streams of thought that they represent.

7. *Collapse,* by Jared Diamond. This big book, a follow-up to Diamond's wildly successful best-seller, *Guns, Germs, and Steel,* is a fascinating look at the ways societies, past and present, choose to fail or to succeed. Environmental choices are at the very heart of success or failure, and Diamond warns again and again, after careful studies of ancient societies from Easter Island to the Anasazi of the American southwest to the Maya of Mexico and Central America, that environmental decisions can

either doom or redeem whole cultures. "Our world is presently on a non-sustainable course, and any of our twelve problems of non-sustainability that we have just summarized would suffice to limit our lifestyle within the next several decades. They are like time bombs with fuses of less than 50 years."[7] The twelve problems are: destruction of natural habitats; loss of wild foods; increasing loss of species; loss of soils; depletion of natural resources; depletion of water; loss of sunlight for photosynthesis; increased toxicity of environments; increased introduction of alien species into new environments; increased release of destructive gases into the atmosphere; population growth; and increased impact of each human on the environment. A preacher should read this wide-ranging book to gain a more expansive and comprehensive view of the problems we are facing environmentally.

8. Several books directly related to the Bible and its reflections on the environment can be listed.

    a. Leo G. Perdue, *Wisdom and Creation*. The thesis of this careful look at the wisdom literature of the Hebrew Bible is "creation theology and its correlative affirmation, providence, were at the center of the sages' understanding of God, the world, and humanity."[8] Perdue examines a wide range of wisdom texts from the Hebrew Bible, connecting them to the theme of creation. A foundational study for anyone who wants to place these particular texts into their wider context in the Bible.

    b. Bill McKibben, *The Comforting Whirlwind: God, Job, and the Scale of Creation*. Here is a rich environmental reading of the speeches of God in the book of Job from a United Methodist activist. There is here great passion and great learning; it is a must for any reading of Job and the natural world.

    c. Theodore Hiebert, *The Yahwist's Landscape: Nature and Religion in Early Israel*. Here is a deeply academic reevaluation of the ways in which nature has been understood by readers of the Bible. In the oldest stratum of the Hebrew Bible, usually named the Yahwist, Hiebert reads the texts again and concludes that the ways their

7. Diamond, *Collapse*, 498.
8. Perdue, *Wisdom and Creation*, 20.

understanding of nature have been portrayed in the scholarly literature is plainly in error. What this study demonstrates is that the Yahwist saw humanity's relationship to nature as servant rather than steward. The importance of this observation may be found in Hiebert's final sentence. "Humanity cannot survive, that is, if it does not recover in some fashion an old sense of humility, as old as the beginnings of Western religious tradition itself. "[9]The reader can readily see how important Hiebert's work has been to my own.

d. William P. Brown, *The Ethos of the Cosmos: The Genesis of Moral Imagination in the Bible*. This is an extraordinarily suggestive book. Brown attempts to show how the portraits of creation in the Hebrew Bible and the New Testament helped to shape the moral character of the ancient communities of faith. For the preacher concerned with the environment the book is not only filled with descriptions of the various ways creation is presented in the texts but also with what the implications for the moral life are contained in those descriptions. In short, Brown does what preachers try always to do, namely, to show the reasons why we should be concerned at all with the actual words of the Scripture, to demonstrate how our lives can be profoundly affected by careful attention to the Bible and its imaginative presentations.

e. Norman Wirzba, *The Paradise of God: Renewing Religion in an Ecological Age*. Here is a delightful book that looks at the Scriptural pictures of creation along with the burgeoning science of modern ecology and finds pictures of a life of peace as envisioned by God. Attention to these pictures will help the world toward a vision of peace that has long escaped us.

f. Terence E. Fretheim, *God and World in the Old Testament: A Relational Theology of Creation*. Every preacher of the environment needs this book. It is a comprehensive attempt to explore just what the Hebrew Bible has to say about creation. The author has a near career-long concern for this issue and has packed into this one volume much of that work. The notes and bibliography are exhaustive but not intrusive. The erudition is exemplary but written in a sparkling prose that carries the reader along. And all along

9. Hiebert, *The Yahwist's Landscape*, 162.

the way, Fretheim offers his understandings of the contemporary implications of his readings of countless texts. An indispensable guide for any preacher concerned about nature and about proclamation based on it.

g. The reader can see that at the head of each of my chapters I have often quoted from two powerful sources of inspiration: Aldo Leopold, *A Sand County Almanac and Other Essays*, and Annie Dillard, *Pilgrim at Tinker Creek*. Each of these modern classics can be read again and again for their lyrical evocations of the natural world along with their wondrous reflections on that world. Both authors teach us to be close observers and deep lovers of what we are seeing. As I have said from the beginning of this book, if one is to be a preacher of the environment, one must first be a lover of it. Leopold and Dillard can be our faithful guides in that loving. Other authors could be named who also write both to inform and to enthuse: Wendell and Thomas Berry, Victor Hanson, and Wes Jackson.[10] And the poet Mary Oliver has many marvelous ways of expressing her love and respect for the nature around her.[11]

h. The Internet is an inexhaustible mine of information and insight about things environmental. A Google search on this and related topics turns up over twenty-five million sites(!), many of which can be valuable sources for the preacher. One thing a quick perusal of just a few of these sites reveals is that concern for the environment is not confined to "liberal tree huggers." A quick check of the National Association of Evangelicals site, for example, reveals deep concern about nature. The NAE has sponsored broad-based meetings on the environment and in October 2004, adopted a document called "For the Health of the Nation: An Evangelical Call to Civic Responsibility," part of which includes a plank on "creation care." (See www.nae.net.) Do not be daunted by the fan-

10. Examples of each author are: Wendell Berry, *Unsettling of America: Culture and Agriculture*, and *Sex, Economy, Freedom, and Community: Eight Essays*; Thomas Berry, *Befriending the Earth: A Theology of Reconciliation Between Humans and the Earth*, and *The Great Work: Our Way into the Future*; Victor Davis Hanson, *Carnage and Culture: Landmark Battles in the Rise of Western Power*; and *Rooted in the Land: Essays on Community and Place*, edited by William Vitek and Wes Jackson.

11. Mary Oliver, *White Pine: Poems and Prose Poems* and *Owls and Other Fantasies: Poems and Essays*.

tastic array of sites to see; be certain you know what your own denomination and/or your local church say publicly about the environment. When preaching on any public issue, there is now simply no excuse for not getting the facts straight. Information is readily available at your fingertips.

Awareness of Those Who Will Hear. Increasing attention in the past few years has been given to the ways in which congregations do, or do not, hear what the preacher is trying to say. When it was thought that the only task the preacher had was to "get it right," that is "right" about what the Bible was saying and "right" about the way the preacher should say it, the congregations were viewed as the passive recipients of the "rightness" of the word of the preacher, the vessels into which the preacher poured the word. This, of course, has never been true about any act of communication, and rhetoricians of the distant past knew it. Still, I have been a teacher of preaching for over twenty-five years, and have taught introductory preaching classes more than fifty times. The bulk of my time in those classes has been given over to getting the content clear and the presentation of that content clear. Our classes have not given much time to the hearers whom we hope will hear. Recent work has turned to the hearers.[12]

Especially when we preach sermons on public issues, we must be aware of various modes of resistance that we will encounter in our hearers. First, some will think that the sermon should not be used for public issue discussion at all, but only for the "gospel," defined narrowly as God's redemption of fallen human beings. Some time may need to be spent in the sermon suggesting why questions of the environment are appropriate in the pulpit at all. Second, some will think that all this environmental talk is scare-mongering by "radical liberals." These hearers may need to hear some hard facts, both from the Bible and from science, before they will deign to pay any attention to such talk. Third, talk about problems is such a "downer" and some listeners will tell you they do not come to church to be told that the world is in trouble. The sermon may have to give some time to suggesting that concern with the environment is God's concern and hence should be ours, too. Thus, God does not always present a smi-

12. Two recent examples are: Joey R. Jeter and Ronald L. Allen, *One Gospel, Many Ears: Preaching for Different Listeners in the Congregation*, and Ronald J. Allen, *Hearing the Sermon: Relationship, Context, Feeling*. The latter is the first of four volumes, the results of a multi-year, multi-denominational study of the listening congregation.

ley face to us, but often challenges us to come out of our smug comfortable certainties and face the world as it is, as we have made it, as opposed to how God has made it.

There is no surprise why public issues preaching is rare in the land. It is hard to do and even harder to do well. Furthermore, few preachers find universal acclamation from parishioners for taking on a controversial public issue. Yet, we preach about such things because they are God's things; we are called to preach by the God who cares about these things as our Bible so clearly reveals to us.

Taking Care of Ourselves. I apologize for placing the care and feeding of the preacher last in my list of necessary actions for anyone who would preach about nature. Yet I suppose there is something horribly ironic in doing so, since concern for ourselves is too often exactly last on the list of things we do to prepare ourselves to preach. When have we last exercised? What have we eaten over the past twenty-four hours? When have we prayed last? Have we visited a therapist or spiritual director recently? When have we last taken a real day off? When did we last genuinely play? You may add to these questions. In my long experience around churches and preachers, I am continually amazed at how poorly we preachers practice self-care.

First, there are our bodies. We are, as a group, too fat, too sedentary, too immobile. Because we are too fat, our breathing is too shallow, our voices are too strained. Because we are too sedentary our stamina is low, our muscles too weak to sustain the hard physical work of preaching. Do not kid yourselves; preaching is hard physical work no matter what regular listeners may think. Whether you pace rapidly, hop around exuberantly, or stay in one spot, you are working physically. For such hard labor we need to be in better shape than we are.

Second, there are our spirits. The work of ministry is emotionally exhausting, especially for those of us who incline a bit toward introversion (the majority of clergy by most accounts). We are called upon daily to pour ourselves out for others, and unless we have genuine reservoirs of pourable stuff, the barrel is always in danger of running dry. Dry barrels become very dangerous in the face of those whose needs are great. Have you ever gone to a pitcher expecting something to slake your raging thirst and found the pitcher empty? How did that empty pitcher make you feel? I urge my students to search out a therapeutic partner, one not only engaged in trying to make you feel good but who is trained to help you see more clearly who you really are, and meet regularly with that person to prevent dry barrel syndrome, the death knell of any ministry. Note: Do not use your spouse or partner for this task!

Third, there are our minds. Ministry is a learned profession, requiring constant thought, constant reflection, constant acquaintance with the ever-changing theological, sociological, political, economic scene. That means one must read, widely and deeply, and constantly. For many of us to get paid to read is a heavenly gift! And, make no mistake; part of what you are paid to do is read. As I have already tried to say, if you are to preach about the environment, careful and wide-ranging reading is a necessity.

Fourth, there are our souls. I have already spoken of the need for prayer, rich conversation with God regularly performed. There are so many different ways to do this prayer to God that it would be presumptuous and foolish of me to tell you how. I only say you need desperately to do so in whatever way that works for you to keep a connection with the one who creates and sustains us all and it all.

I urge you to preach about God's nature, God's environment, made whole by the gift of Jesus Christ. No more important subject for your preaching can be chosen in this new century. There is no doubt that we all, human, animal, and plant, face catastrophe unless we make some fundamental changes in viewpoint and in action. I am nearly sixty-five years old. The probability is that my life will end before any drastically different environmental realities are clearly in evidence. (Although some startling pictures of the loss of glaciers over the past one hundred years in Glacier National Park appeared this week in my local newspaper. In 1900 there were well over one hundred glaciers readily observed in the park. Now there are fewer than twenty. Recent glacier studies suggest that there will be no glaciers in the park easily seen by 2075. What will we rename the park if the glaciers disappear altogether?) My children are thirty-seven and thirty-three years old. They, I hope, will live at least fifty more years. What will they see by 2061? Will the rain forests be almost gone? Will the global temperature be two degrees centigrade warmer, bringing about a two- to three-foot rise in the oceans? Much of Bangladesh, one of the world's most impoverished places, will be permanently under water. On our own coasts, many buildings will need to be moved or demolished.

What will my children's children see? By the year 2120 what will our world be like? We are not in the realm of science fiction, but in the realm of facts that will be quite terrible without significant change.

It is far past time for us to see the world as it really is, not as we always assumed it was or as we assumed it always would be. We preachers need to join the chorus of the earth in praise to God and in protest against those of us who would needlessly destroy the good earth and its creatures given to us so freely and lovingly by our creator. It is not too late for our conversion to become lovers of and partners with God's world. But we must be honest; it is surely getting very late.

Bibliography

Allen, Ronald J. *Hearing the Sermon: Relationship, Context, Feeling.* St. Louis: Chalice, 2004.

Atwood, Margaret. *Oryx and Crake.* New York: Doubleday, 2003.

Aune, David H. *Revelation.* Waco, TX: Word, 1997–98.

Balabanski, Vicky. "John 1—the Earth Bible Challenge: An Extra-textual Approach to Reading John 1." In *The Earth Story in the New Testament,* edited by Norman C. Habel and Vicky Balabanski, 89–94. Cleveland: The Pilgrim Press, 2002.

Barth, Karl. *Letters 1961–1968.* Translated by Geoffrey W. Bromiley. Grand Rapids: Eerdmans, 1981.

Berry, Thomas. *Befriending the Earth: A Theology of Reconciliation Between Humans and the Earth.* Mystic, Conn: Twenty-Third Publications, 1991.

_____. *The Great Work: Our Way into the Future.* New York: Bell Tower, 1999.

Berry, Wendell. *The Unsettling of America: Culture and Agriculture.* San Francisco: Sierra Club, 1977.

_____. *Sex, Economy, Freedom, and Community.* New York: Pantheon, 1993.

Betz, Hans Dieter. *Sermon on the Mount.* Minneapolis: Fortress, 1995.

The Bible and Culture Collective, *The Postmodern Bible.* New Haven: Yale University Press, 1995.

Blount, Brian K. *Revelation.* Louisville: Westminster John Knox, 2009.

Boff, Leonardo. *Ecology and Liberation.* Translated by John Cumming. Maryknoll, NY: Orbis, 1995.

Bornkamm, Gunther. *Paul.* Translated by D.M.G. Stalker. New York: Harper & Row, 1971.

Boring, M. Eugene. *Revelation.* Louisville: John Knox, 1989.

Bouma-Prediger, Steven. *For the Beauty of the Earth: A Christian Vision for Creation Care.* Grand Rapids: Baker, 2001.

Boyer, Paul. *When Time Shall Be No More.* Cambridge: Oxford University Press, 1992.

Brown, Raymond. *The Gospel According to John.* New York: Doubleday, 1966.

Brown, William P. *The Ethics of the Cosmos: The Genesis of Moral Imagination in the Bible.* Grand Rapids: Eerdmans, 1999.

Caird, G. B. *The Revelation of St. John the Divine.* New York: Harper & Row, 1966.

Carmichael, C. M. *The Story of Creation: Its Origin and Interpretation in Philo and the Fourth Gospel.* Ithaca, NY: Cornell University Press, 1996.

Carson, D. A. *The Gospel According to John.* Grand Rapids: Eerdmans, 1991.

Carstensen, R. W. *Job, Defense of Honor.* Nashville, TN: Abingdon, 1963.

Bibliography

Cobb, John B., Jr. *Is It Too Late? A Theology of Ecology*. Beverly Hills, CA: Benziger, Bruce, and Glencoe, 1972.

Cousar, Charles B., *The Letters of Paul*. Nashville, TN: Abingdon, 1996.

Cullmann, Oscar. *Christ and Time*. Translated by Floyd V. Filson. Philadelphia, PA: Westminster, 1950.

Diamond, Jared. *Collapse*. New York: Viking, 2005.

Dillard, Annie. *Pilgrim at Tinker Creek*. New York: Bantam, 1975.

Driver, Samuel Roles, and John Gray. *The Book of Job*. Edinburgh: T &T Clark, 1921.

Flor, Elmer. "The Cosmic Christ and Ecojustice in the New Testament (Ephesians 1)." In *The Earth Story in the New Testament*, edited by Norman C. Habel and Vicky Balabanski, 137–47. Cleveland: Pilgrim, 2002.

Fretheim, Terence E. *God and World in the Old Testament: A Relational Theology of Creation*. Nashville, TN: Abingdon, 2005.

Friedman, Thomas L. *Hot, Flat, and Crowded*. New York: Farrar, Strauss & Giroux, 2008.

Furnish, Victor Paul. "The Letter of Paul to the Ephesians." In *The Interpreter's One-Volume Commentary on the Bible*. Edited by Charles M. Laymon. Nashville, TN: Abingdon, 1971.

_____. "The Letter of Paul to the Colossians." In *The Interpreter's One-Volume Commentary on the Bible*. Edited by Charles M. Laymon. Nashville, TN: Abingdon, 1971.

Habel, Norman. *Job*. Philadelphia, PA: Westminster, 1985.

_____. "An Ecojustice Challenge: Is Earth Valued in John 1?" In *The Earth Story in the New Testament*, edited by Norman C. Habel and Vicky Balabanski, 76-82. Cleveland: Pilgrim, 2002.

_____. *An Inconvenient Text*. Adelaide: ATF Press, 2009.

Hanson, Victor David. *Rooted in the Land: Essays on Community and Place*. Edited by William Vitek and Wes Jackson. New Haven: Yale University Press, 1996.

_____. *Carnage and Culture: Landmark Battles in the Rise of Western Power*. New York: Anchor, 2002.

Hertsgaard, Mark. *Hot: Living Through the Next Fifty Years on Earth*. Boston: Houghton Mifflin Harcourt, 2011.

Hiebert, Theodore. *The Yahwist's Landscape: Nature and Religion in Early Israel*. New York: Oxford University Press, 1996.

Holbert, John C. "The Bible Becomes Literature: An Encounter with Ruth," *Word & World*. Vol. 13, No. 2, Spring, 1993, 130–35.

Jeter, Joey R., and Ronald L. Allen. *One Gospel, Many Ears: Preaching for Different Listeners in the Congregation*. St. Louis: Chalice, 2002.

The Jewish Study Bible. Edited by Michael Fishbane. New York: Oxford University Press, 1999.

LaHaye, Tim and Jerry B. Jenkins. *Left Behind*. Carol Stream, IL: Tyndale House, 2005.

Leopold, Aldo. *The Quality of Landscape*. New York: Ballantine, 1966.

_____. *Essays on Conservation from Round River*. New York: Ballantine, 1970.

_____. *A Sand County Almanac*. New York: Ballantine, 1966.

Leska, Adrian M. "Matthew 6:25–34: Human Anxiety and the Natural World." In *The Earth Story in the New Testament*, edited by Norman C. Habel and Vicky Balabanski, 15–27. Cleveland: Pilgrim, 2002.

Lindsey, Hal. *The Late Great Planet Earth*. Grand Rapids: Zondervan, 1970.

McGrath, Alister. *The Reenchantment of Nature*. New York: Doubleday, 2002.

McKane, William. *Proverbs*. Philadelphia, PA: Westminster, 1970.

McKenzie, Roderick A. F. "The Purpose of the Yahweh Speeches in the Book of Job," *Biblica*, 40 (1959) 435–445.

McKibben, Bill. *The End of Nature*. New York: Random House, 1989.

_____. *The Comforting Whirlwind: God, Job, and the Scale of Creation*. Grand Rapids: Eerdmans, 1994.

Mayes, James Luther. *Amos*. Philadelphia, PA: Westminster, 1969.

Morris, Leon. *The Gospel According to John*. Grand Rapids: Eerdmans, 1995.

Moule, C.F.D. "The Letter of Paul to the Colossians," in *Peake's Commentary on the Bible*. London: Thomas Nelson, 1962.

Oliver, Mary. *White Pine: Poems and Prose Poems*. New York: Harcourt Brace, 1994.

_____. *Owls and Other Fantasies: Poems and Essays*. Boston: Beacon, 2003.

Perdue, Leo G. *Wisdom and Creation*. Nashville, TN: Abingdon, 1994.

Pope, Marvin H. *Job*. Garden City: Doubleday, 1973.

Ridderbos, Herman N. *The Gospel According to John*. Grand Rapids: Eerdmans, 1997.

Roetzel, Calvin. *Paul: The Man and the Myth*. Minneapolis: Fortress, 1999.

Santmire, H. Paul. *Brother Earth: Nature, God, and Ecology in a Time of Crisis*. New York: Thomas Nelson, 1970.

_____. *The Travail of Nature: The Ambiguous Ecological Promise in Christian Theology*. Philadelphia: Fortress, 1985.

_____. *Nature Reborn: The Ecological and Cosmic Promise of Christian Theology*. Minneapolis: Augsburg Fortress, 2000.

Schüssler-Fiorenza, Elizabeth. *The Book of Revelation: Justice and Judgment*. Philadelphia: Fortress, 1985.

Sittler, Joseph. *Essays on Nature and Grace*. Philadelphia: Fortress, 1972.

Speth, James Gustave. *Red Sky at Morning*. New Haven: Yale University Press, 2005.

Trible, Phyllis. *God and the Rhetoric of Sexuality*. Philadelphia: Fortress, 1978.

The United Methodist Hymnal. Edited by Carlton R. Young. Nashville, TN: The United Methodist Publishing House, 1989.

Ward, James M. *Amos and Isaiah*. Nashville, TN: Abingdon, 1969.

_____. *Thus Says the Lord*. Nashville, TN: Abingdon, 1991.

Weber, Timothy P. *Living in the Shadow of the Second Coming*. New York: Oxford University Press, 1979.

_____. *On the Road to Armageddon*. Grand Rapids: Baker, 2004.

White, Jr., Lynn. "The Historical Roots of Our Ecological Crisis." *Science* 155 (1967), 1203–1207.

Wirzba, Norman. *The Paradise of God: Renewing Religion in an Ecological Age*. New York: Oxford University Press, 2003.